The
POETRY
of
JOHN LYDGATE

The POETRY *of* JOHN LYDGATE

by

ALAIN RENOIR

HARVARD UNIVERSITY PRESS
Cambridge, Massachusetts
1967

Printed in Great Britain

CONTENTS

	PREFACE	*page* VII
I.	OPINIONS ABOUT LYDGATE	1
II.	THE OPINIONS RECONSIDERED	13
III.	THE PERIOD OF TRANSITION	32
IV.	THE MEDIAEVAL TRADITION	46
V.	CLASSICAL ANTIQUITY	61
VI.	THE PARAGON OF ANIMALS	74
VII.	THE NATION AND THE PRINCE	95
VIII.	THE STORY OF THEBES	110
IX.	ANOTHER POINT OF VIEW	136
	NOTES	145
	INDEX	167

PREFACE

ÉMILE ZOLA is said to have remarked that if he could not overwhelm by his talent he would overwhelm by his quantity. With more than 140,000 verses to his credit, John Lydgate is unquestionably an overwhelming poet. Because he was not only the most productive but also the most versatile writer of fifteenth-century England, because he translated into English such monuments of Continental literature as Guido delle Colonne's *Historia* and Giovanni Boccaccio's *De Casibus*, and because his lifetime extended over a period of great interest to students of the English language, his works have been the object of extensive historical and philological investigation. Because of his quasi-proverbial dullness, however, his production has remained all but untouched by modern literary criticism. To be sure, histories of English literature abound with contemptuous opinions of him, but these almost always originate from critics who have demonstrably failed to read seriously the materials they are criticizing.

A total reassessment of Lydgate's production is a task for neither one book nor one man. The book would necessarily be as voluminous and boring as its subject-matter is assumed to be; and no one man can present more than what is in effect his personal opinion. To be convincing, the reassessment of any substantial body of literature must be the work of several literary critics writing from their respective points of view and evaluating all the principal aspects of the material in the light of their several areas of competence. The cumulative verdict of such a jury is the only evaluation which the literary public may accept as something more than a personal opinion. Although the present study attempts to evaluate the outstanding aspects of Lydgate's poetry, it has no pretention to being a final reassessment. My purpose is simply to present as convincing an argument as I can muster in favour of such a reassessment by several hands, as well as to suggest what results may be expected from serious critical examination of Lydgate's poetry. The conclusion is that unprejudiced examination will reveal Lydgate to be neither the master whom his own age saw in him nor the contemptible bore whom our age sees in him, but rather a competent craftsman who occasionally rises to a high level of poetic felicity. If the present study prompts the reader to turn to Lydgate with an unprejudiced mind, my purpose will have been accomplished.

Much of my argument depends on the contention that Lydgate is not so exclusively typical of the Middle Ages as literary critics and historians have hitherto assumed, but often exhibits traits which we have been taught to associate with the Renaissance. Because this is a work of literary criticism rather than of historical definition, the terms 'Middle Ages' and 'Renaissance' are used whenever possible in the sense in which they are commonly understood by modern students of literature. In discussing the literary quality of Lydgate's poetry, it matters very little whether he was really a man of the Middle Ages or really a man of the Renaissance; but it matters very much whether we should look at him as we look upon the Middle Ages or as we look upon the Renaissance, however mistaken we may be in our conception of these historical periods.

With a few exceptions, the texts examined here have been selected from Lydgate's secular works. The exclusion of his religious poetry does not imply a negative judgment, but merely my own limitations and my reluctance to obscure the argument with theological considerations which apply only to a large but very special segment of Lydgate's production. I have thought it best to adhere to the Lydgate canon established by Henry N. MacCracken in *The Minor Poems of Lydgate* (I, xi–xxxi) and reprinted with commentary by Walter F. Schirmer in *John Lydgate: Ein Kulturbild aus dem 15. Jahrhundert* (pp. 228 ff.), because it is accepted by a majority of scholars. The Mac-

Cracken-Schirmer list, however, must necessarily remain tentative in certain respects, for it is not always possible to distinguish Lydgate's more conventional pieces from those of anonymous imitators. This caution applies especially to his courtly poems; in *Sir Richard Roos* (e.g. pp. 125 ff.), for instance, Ethel Seaton has recently argued in favour of attributing a majority of these to Richard Roos—along with the *Legend of Good Women* and a quantity of poems usually attributed to Chaucer, Suffolk, and Wyatt. For this reason, I have centred my own argument upon the three great works unequivocally attributed to Lydgate: the *Troy Book*, the *Fall of Princes*, and the *Siege of Thebes*. I have not, however, completely disregarded the poems rejected by Professor Seaton, but her impressive theory is far from having gained general acceptance, and my purpose is to discuss Lydgate as he is normally accepted today rather than as one scholar would have him.

In quoting from Lydgate and other late Middle English texts, I have followed the example of modern editors of Chaucer in substituting modern symbols for the *ȝ* and þ of diplomatic editions and printing all characters according to current practice as often as possible. I have likewise modernized the punctuation whenever advisable for the sake of clarity. Since this study is not concerned with textual problems, I have not reproduced the various indications of editorial emendations; and I have used brackets and footnotes to indicate my own departures from the editions cited when the changes are other than orthographical. Because Lydgate is not consistent in his use of the definite article in titles, and refers to 'the Siege of Thebes' on the one hand but to 'Troy Book' on the other, I have arbitrarily omitted it in italicized titles, and have written both 'the *Siege of Thebes*' and 'the *Troy Book*'. I have departed from this practice only in the rare instances where inclusion of the article is required by the grammar.

The references in my work will reveal the extent of my indebtedness to previous Lydgate scholars. I owe a more immediate, though less obvious debt to Professors Harry T. Levin, Francis P. Magoun, jun., and Bartlett J. Whiting, of Harvard University, for their generous advice especially in respect to my treatment of the Theban Legend. I am grateful to Professors

Bertrand Evans and Robert L. McNulty, of the University of California (Berkeley), for the constant encouragement and help which the former gave me and for the relentlessly acute criticism with which the latter forced me to reconsider many of my views. For suggestions too numerous to receive individual acknowledgments, I am grateful to the late James J. Lynch and to Professors Willard Farnham, Ernest Tuveson, and Larzer Ziff, also of the University of California (Berkeley). I also wish to thank Professors Germaine Brée, Marshall Clagett, and Helen C. White, of the University of Wisconsin, for an invitation to the Institute for Research in the Humanities which has freed me from time-consuming academic duties while working on the present study of Lydgate's poetry. Finally, I wish to acknowledge the courtesy of the editors of *Convivium*, *English Miscellany*, and *English Studies* for their permission to reproduce with substantial changes sections of essays previously published in these journals.

ALAIN RENOIR

Chapter One

OPINIONS ABOUT LYDGATE

JOHN LYDGATE (1370?–1450?)[1] was born near the close of the Middle Ages and died on the eve of the English Renaissance, after having spent some sixty-six years as a monk of the Benedictine abbey of Bury Saint Edmunds. He was one of the most prolific poets of all ages, and unquestionably the most important of his own time and country. During his mature lifetime and for more than three hundred years afterwards, his countrymen ranked him on a level with the greatest poets; today, he is generally despised as one of the dullest versifiers[2] in the English language. The completeness of the change may be illustrated by the juxtaposition of two opinions concerning his poetry. The first is from John Metham's *Amoryus and Cleopes*, finished about 1458–9:

> Eke Jon Lydgate, sumtyme monke off Byry,
> Hys bokys endytyd with termys off retoryk
> And halff chongyd Latyne, with conseytys off poetry
> And craffty imagynacionys off thingys fantastyk;
> But eke hys qwyght her schewyd, and hys late werk,
> How that hys contynwauns made hym both a poyet and a clerk.[3]

The second is from H. S. Bennett's *Six Medieval Men and Women*, published in 1955, and is limited to a single word with which much of the poet's production is summarily dismissed: 'verbiage'.[4]

Metham's opinion was without a doubt shared by the

English literary public of the fifteenth century. The number and diversity of patrons for whom Lydgate wrote bear witness to the high respect in which his contemporaries held his talent: they were both men and women, the Church and the laity, the kings and the nobility of England, the Lord Mayor of London and the great craft guilds.[5] The range and variety of the pieces which he produced at their request indicate that they expected him to succeed in almost every mode of composition: his works include monumental epics and eight-line prayers, philosophical treatises and lives of saints, love poems and dietaries.[6] In addition, the number of extant manuscripts makes it clear that, even if no single work of his ever enjoyed the unrivalled popularity of the *Canterbury Tales*, his reputation must have been second only to that of Chaucer. Rossell Hope Robbins and Carleton Brown, for instance, record twenty-six manuscripts of his *Siege of Thebes*, twenty-four of his *Fall of Princes*, and twelve containing excerpts of the latter work; but only seventeen of Chaucer's *Troilus and Criseyde*, fifteen of his *Parliament of Fowls*, and twelve of his *Legend of Good Women*.[7]

Much may be inferred from the fact that Lydgate's works were among the very first pieces of English literature to go to the printing press and were still on the market as late as the second half of the sixteenth century. Among others, his *Temple of Glas* was printed by William Caxton as early as 1477, only a year after Chaucer's *Parliament* and five years before his *Troilus*, and was reprinted twice—by Wynkyn de Worde in 1498 and by Richard Pynson, probably in 1500—before either of these two went to its second printing. His *Fall of Princes*, which had originally been printed by Pynson in 1494, was still being reprinted by Richard Tottell in 1554, and again by John Wayland the year after. Likewise, his *Siege of Thebes*, which de Worde had first printed about 1500, was being included by John Stowe in his 1561 *Chaucer*, almost a century after the first of Lydgate's works to go through the press had been issued by Caxton. The significance of these considerations becomes obvious if we keep in mind that, unlike manuscript scribes, the early printers could not afford to limit their production of a given work to a few copies intended to be read by a scholar or to adorn the library of a wealthy patron.[8] Like their modern colleagues, they were engaged in a business venture whose financial success depended on mass production; accordingly, the books which they would print and reprint had to be those which the public would buy in sufficient quantity to justify the expense of setting the fonts. We know that Caxton's editions, for example, numbered several hundred copies each,[9] and such quantities must have seemed as overwhelming to his contemporaries as they seem insignificant today.

My reasoning does not imply that Lydgate's popularity after the advent of printing was with the general public only. On the contrary, as his works became easily available, the world of letters began reiterating its praises with renewed energy. Walter F. Schirmer, the foremost Lydgatian today, reminded us a few years ago that literary critics consistently uttered the name of Lydgate in the same breath with those of Chaucer and Gower until the beginning of the seventeenth century.[10] The practice may have been partly conventional,[11] but the frequency of its occurrence does not allow us to dismiss it as irrelevant. About 1508, we find John Skelton paying him a singular compliment with the assertion that there exists 'No man that can amend/Those maters that he hath pende', and noting, with what I take to be mild astonishment, that 'Yet some men find a faute/And say he writeth too haut.'[12] The very conventional address to Henry VII with which Stephen Hawes opens *The Pastime of Pleasure*, completed in 1509, is indicative of the qualities which the early Renaissance saw in the works of Lydgate:

Your noble grace and excellent hyenes
For to accepte I beseche ryght humbly
This lytell boke apprest with rudeness
Without rethorycke or colour crafty.
Nothynge I am experte in poetry
As the monke of Bury, flour of eloquence,
Which was in tyme of grete ecellence,
Of your predecessour the .v. kynge Henry,
Unto whose grace he dyde present
Ryght famous bokes of parfyte memory,
Of his faynynge with termes eloquent
Whose fatall fyccyons are yet permanent
Grounded on reason with clowdy figures

He cloked the trouthe of all his scriptures.
. . . . .
Besechynge your grace to pardon myne ignoraunce,
Whyche this fayned fable to eschewe ydlenesse
Have so compyled now without doubtance
For to present to your hye worthynesse,
Of my Mayster Lydgate with due exercise
Suche fayned tales I do fynde and devyse.[13]

Although Lydgate's monastic calling had little to recommend him to the Reformation, his reputation continued unabated during the Elizabethan period and the later Renaissance. Thus, his poetry is offered as an example of the very best style in Richard Sherry's *Treatise of Schemes and Tropes* (f. Aii^{b}), published in 1550; and in 1559, John Bale rates him first among the early English poets, commends him on almost all possible counts, and concludes, 'This man was of such great eloquence and erudition that we can never admire him enough.'[14] As may be expected, even his most ardent admirers after the Reformation found it occasionally necessary to apologize for his profession and for the Roman Catholicism that necessarily permeated his lives of saints. This mixture of aesthetic approval and religious suspicion is evident in John Lawson's *Orchet*, published in 1581:

I tooke Maister *John Lidgaite* strighte then in my hande
With whome the reste of my tyme I thought to leede:
Whose wordye praise and everlastynge meade,
Thoo he war a mounke at the abbay late Bury,
Mighte be in equale prase with Maister *Chaucer* truly.[15]

A similar attitude expressed in greater detail pervades the comparison between Lydgate and Chaucer which William Webbe included five years later in *A Discourse on English Poetry*:

Neere in time unto him was *Lydgate* a poet, surely for good proportion of his verse and meetely currant style, as the time affoorded comparable to Chaucer, yet more occupyed in superticious and odde matters then was requisite in so good a wytte: which, though he handled them commendably, yet the matters themselves beeing not so commendable, hys estimation hath been the lesse.[16]

The opinion which the Elizabethans had of Lydgate is perhaps best summed up by George Puttenham when he simply calls him 'one that wrate in good verse'.[17]

Students of literary history often assume that Lydgate was practically forgotten during the seventeenth century.[18] One may wonder, however, whether the lack of extant criticism is strong enough evidence to justify the assumption. The fact that Thomas Heywood's *Iron Age* is based on Lydgate's *Troy Book* suggests that the poet's reputation was still holding its own a little before the Closing of the Theatres. If his name was ever really forgotten during the Commonwealth it was only to come out again with the dawn of the eighteenth century, when sophisticated men of letters went on reading and discussing his works. Beginning with 1707, when an anonymous contributor to *The Muses Mercury* ranked him above Chaucer himself,[19] Lydgate is repeatedly likened and occasionally preferred to the older poet, under whose tutelage he was thought to have learned the craft of poetry. In 1754, Theophilus Cibber writes, 'he was a disciple and admirer of Chaucer, and it must be owned far excelled his master in the article of versification'.[20] The same year, Thomas Warton discusses Lydgate's account of the marriage of Oedipus as something which 'Chaucer cannot surpass'.[21] Some ten years later, we shall find him summing up the poet's contribution as follows:

> He was a monk of the Benedictine abbey of Bury in Suffolk, and an uncommon ornament of his profession. Yet his genius was so lively, and his accomplishments so numerous, that I suppose the holy father saint Benedict would hardly have acknowledged him for a genuine disciple. . . . On the whole I am of the opinion that Lydgate made considerable additions to those amplifications of our language, in which Chaucer, Gower, and Occleve led the way: and that he is the first of our writers whose style is clothed with that perspicuity in which the English phraseology appears at this day to an English reader. . . . No poet seems to have possessed a greater versatility of talents.[22]

Warton may be considered the last representative of an age that simply took for granted that anything composed by Lydgate had to be excellent. In one respect he is similar to nearly all the critics who preceded him: he never cites specific examples of the qualities which he praises so highly in the material under discussion. Except for his open dislike of Roman Catholic monks and of what he terms the 'barbarism' (p. 51) of the poets who immediately followed Chaucer, we might be tempted to accept Isaac D'Israeli's accusation that he was merely paying lip service to 'a Gothic monk composing ancient romances'.[23]

The one outstanding exception to the uncritical attitude of Lydgate's admirers from the fifteenth to the eighteenth century is Thomas Gray. In his essay, 'On the Poems of Lydgate', published in 1760, he takes pains to examine the *Fall of Princes* before reaching a verdict that is both complimentary and reasonable: 'I do not pretend to set him on a level with his master, Chaucer, but he certainly comes the nearest to him of any contemporary writer that I am acquainted with. His choice of expression, and the smoothness of his verse, far surpass both Gower and Occleve.'[24] It is worth noting that, unlike his predecessors, Gray shows an acute awareness of the tendency toward prolixity which modern critics have since found the most objectionable aspect of Lydgate's poetry. Unlike them, however, he sees in it no cause for censure, and dismisses it as a stylistic characteristic shared by many poets, including Homer himself.

For the purpose of the present investigation, we may say that the first significant adverse criticism of Lydgate was published by Thomas Percy in 1765. In one of the essays included in the *Reliques of Ancient English Poetry*, Percy mentions 'the dull and prolix legends of Lydgate',[25] and argues that the real reason for that poet's enduring reputation is that 'the antiquaries, who have revived the works of our ancient writers, have been for the most part men devoid of taste and genius . . . who have been careful to grub up every petty fragment of the most dull and insipid rhimist, whose merit it was to deform morality, or to obscure true history' (*ibid.*).

It was not, however, until the beginning of the nineteenth century that Lydgate fell into complete disrepute with the overwhelming majority of English-speaking critics; and the publication in 1802 of Joseph Ritson's *Bibliographia Poetica* may well be responsible for the subsequent and lasting fashion of sneering at a poet who, as Sharon Turner observed, 'has been oftener abused than read'.[26] Ritson had already declared, in 1783, that 'Dan John, like most of the professed poets of that age, laboured too much with a leaden pen'.[27] In *Bibliographia Poetica* he picks up and develops Percy's suggestion that Lydgate is both dull and prolix. With his customary verbal pugnacity he sketches his victim as 'a most prolix and voluminous poetaster' (p. 66) and 'a voluminous, prosaic, and driveling monk' (p. 87). He then goes on to compare him with Chaucer, and the result is his categorical pronouncement that the younger poet is no poet at all:

> But, in truth, and in fact, these stupid and fatigueing productions, which by no means deserve the name of poetry, and their still more stupid and disgusting author, who disgraces the name and patronage of his master Chaucer, are neither worth collecting . . . nor even worthy of preservation: being only suitably adapted '*ad ficum & piperem*', and other more base and servile uses. How little he profited by the correction, or instructions of his great patron is manifest in almost every part of his elaborate drawlings, in which there are scarcely three lines together of pure and accurate metre. (p. 88)

D'Israeli, himself no admirer of Lydgate, has pertinently remarked, 'Ritson, whose rabid hostility to the clerical character was part of his constitutional malady, . . . hints at the "cart-loads of rubbish of a voluminous poetaster; a prosaick and driveling monk". And this is speedily seized upon by the hand of the bibliographers.'[28] If indeed Ritson be the real originator of the current attitude of literary critics toward Lydgate, his conscious or unconscious followers are many and vociferous. Some of them, like Thomas Dibdin, are content to relegate Lydgate's poetry to the museum, along with the crossbow and the breastplate: 'Lydgate is rather food for the Antiquary than the general reader.'[29] Most of them, however, enlarge complacently upon defects which they rarely illustrate specifically, and not infrequently make their criticism an excuse for exercising their wit at the expense of the author whom they are supposedly discussing. Thus, in 1801 we read of the *Siege of Thebes* that 'Lydgate's poem is not long, but it is possible to be tedious in a very small compass'.[30] In 1899 one critic wryly states, 'if an author could claim greatness by the fertility of his pen, Lydgate ought to be classed among the first in rank. . . . Unfortunately, the quality does not match the number of verses.'[31] In 1903 another facetiously sighs, 'we may well grumble at the mischance which has preserved such quantities of the verse of men like Lydgate . . .',[32] and in 1907 yet another pretends to thank the luck that has befallen him, 'two whole folios of a poem by Lydgate being mercifully missing'.[33] Of course, not all critics have been inspired to such witticisms, so that we find the poet's favourite metre bluntly dismissed in 1910 as 'an arrangement of extraordinary hideousness, which occurs rather frequently in Lydgate',[34] and one of his best-known poems cited in 1951 as illustrating 'Dan John's prodigious gift for twaddle'.[35]

In keeping with its aim of outlining the course of Lydgate's reputation, the preceding survey has necessarily simplified matters: in effect there were occasional late-mediaeval and Renaissance men of letters who disapproved of Lydgate, and there are occasional modern critics who approve of him. I have already cited Skelton's mention of unsympathetic critics, and we should note here that Lydgate's own contemporary, William de la Pole, seems to have been so incensed at certain passages in the *Fall of Princes* that he could not forbear giving public expression to his displeasure:

> Thy corupt speche enfectyth alle the air.
>
> . . . . .
>
> O thou, unhappy man, go hyde thy face.
> The court ys set, thy falshed is tryed;
> Withdraw, I rede, for now thow art aspyed.[36]

Yet, his resentment did not prevent him from expressing in unequivocal terms his admiration for the artistry of the man whom he was so vigorously censuring:

> And to the, Monke of Bury, now speke I,
> Ffor thy connyng ys syche, and eke thy grace,
> After Chaucer to occupye his place. (26–28)

In 1625 Henry Peacham reproaches Lydgate with 'having no great invention',[37] and a little over a hundred years afterwards

Elizabeth Cooper tells us how she approached his works with great expectations and found them utterly unreadable.[38]

Among the critics who have expressed approval of Lydgate since the eighteenth century, we may cite Richard Thompson, who in 1827 calls one of his poems 'but little less beautiful than Chaucer's immortal Tales'[39] and rejects Ritson's verdict as 'malignant and untrue' (p. 277). In 1896, Mary Augusta Scott admits Lydgate to the company of the 'poets who have "lifted the thoughts of Man" ',[40] and in our own time H. S. Bennett himself has somewhat reluctantly recognized that he must be considered the 'outstanding poet of the fifteenth-century England'.[41] Possibly the most sympathetic verdict to come from a recent English-speaking critic is a passing remark by Ethel Seaton, who objects to Lydgate's heavy ornateness but notes 'his occasional solid impressiveness'.[42]

Because the detractors of Lydgate have been so loud and numerous, some critics have felt called upon to come forth with sober evaluations. However, their well-meaning attempts to say something good about him have proved perhaps more damaging than Ritson's thunder. The case of Edmund Gosse, who wrote around the beginning of the present century, will illustrate the point. Although Gosse believes that Lydgate 'had a brisker talent than Occleve',[43] he carefully warns us that 'the excessive prolixity and uniformity of his style, which never rises and cannot fall, baffles all but the most persistent reader' (p. 36). The qualities which he culls from Lydgate's verse are not likely to encourage anyone to read it:

> It is not probable that the entire works of Lydgate will ever be made accessible to readers, nor is it to be conceived that they would reward the labours of an editor. But although it must be repeated that Lydgate is an author of inferior value, excessively prosy and long-winded, and strangely neglectful both of structure and melody, a selection could probably be made of his writings which would do him greater justice than he does to himself in his intolerable prolixity. He has a pleasant vein of human pity, a sympathy with suffering that leads him to say, in a sort of deprecating overtone, very gentle and gracious things. He is a storehouse of odd and valuable antiquarian notes. (pp. 36–37)

Considering the opinions examined above, we need not wonder that modern editors of Lydgate have at times felt compelled to apologize for undertaking their labours,[44] or that Schirmer himself must cautiously admit, 'war Lydgate keine überragende Dichterpersönlichkeit'.[45] We may, however, wonder a little more at Elizabeth Barrett Browning's statement that Lydgate has been 'much overrated by the critics'.[46]

Earlier in this chapter I expressed my agreement with Sharon Turner's belief that Lydgate has been more often abused than read. The cases of Thomas Lounsbury and George Saintsbury will bear out the point.

Lounsbury's criticism of Lydgate is probably the nastiest since Ritson's:

> He produced . . . a good deal of matter which it presumably gratified him to write; though it is inconceivable that there was ever a state of human intellect in which gratification could have come to anyone from its perusal. In his versification there is no harmony, no regular movement. In his expression, he has gained facility at the expense of felicity. . . . There is, accordingly, no necessity of reading his works resting upon any one save him who has to make a professional study of English literature. For this unfortunate being the dead past, so far from being able to bury its dead, is not even able to bury its bores.[47]

Like the majority of critics since the beginning of the nineteenth century, Lounsbury assumes that Lydgate is dull; and his vituperous antagonism seems partly due to a curious conviction that the poet spent his life in sordid attempts to hide this blemish:

> Lydgate was dull, and he probably never knew it. He certainly never told of it, if he did know it. The wise reticence he displayed in refraining to commit himself upon the point to his own disadvantage has been rewarded a hundred fold. He was accepted and is even now occasionally accepted at a valuation which was put upon him at a period when there was not a sufficient quantity of literature in the language to make men very discriminating about its quality. (p. 24)

We need not surmise whether an author should be expected to make public acknowledgments of his own dullness, real as it may be. We must note, however, that it is impossible to read more than a few lines of his poetry without finding Lydgate apologizing over and over again for the inadequacies which he constantly sees in his own works. Furthermore, he repeatedly uses Lounsbury's own word—*dull*—in doing so. In the *Troy Book*,[48] for example, he laments his being too 'dulle' (II, 169) to do justice to Guido delle Colonne's Latin, and he begs our forgiveness for his own 'dul stille' (III, 5763); at the outset of the *Siege of Thebes*,[49] he warns us that his wit 'barayn be and dul' (183), and at the end of *Guy of Warwyck*[50] he asks the potentially dissatisfied reader not to blame the story but rather to 'put the wyte for dulnesse on Lydgate' (584). Even if we dismiss these apologies for dullness as purely conventional expressions of what professional mediaevalists have termed the topos of affected modesty,[51] we may reasonably suspect Lounsbury's reading of having been somewhat more casual than his tone of final authority would imply.

Saintsbury lays himself open to the same kind of suspicion. In *The Cambridge History of English Literature* he reproaches Lydgate with 'longwinded prolixity' (II, 228) and concludes with the following summation of his alleged vices:

> But what is most fatal of all is the flatness of diction noticed above—the dull, hackneyed, slovenly phraseology, only thrown up by his occasional aureate pedantry—which makes the common commoner and the uncommon uninteresting. Lydgate himself or some imitator of him, has been credited with the phrase 'gold dewdrops of speech' about Chaucer. He would hardly have thought of anything so good; but the phrase at least suggests an appropriate variant, 'leaden splashes', for his own. (II, 234)

For the purpose of the present argument, it is a significant coincidence that the phrase 'gold dewdrops of speech' not only *does* occur in Lydgate's poetry, but that it appears in one of the very best and most famous passages of his *Life of Our Lady*—a work to which Saintsbury has devoted almost an entire page of the *Cambridge History*:

> And eke my maister Chauser is ygrave,
> The noble rethor, poete of Brytayne
> That worthy was the laurer to have

> Of poetrye, and the palme atteyne,
> That made firste to distille and rayne
> The *golde dewedropes of speche* and eloquence
> Into our tunge, thurgh his excellence.[52]

These are not such lines as a critical reader may overlook, especially if we consider that the encomium of Chaucer continues on the same level of poetic excellence for three more stanzas. Nor must we forget that Lydgate uses a very similar expression—'The gold dewedropis of rhetorik so fyne'—in *Troy Book* (II, 4699), a work also discussed in the *Cambridge History*. The coincidence mentioned here suggests that Saintsbury's Olympian contempt for Lydgate may have been at least partially the result of his own lack of objectivity in reading the materials which he was so articulately damning.

The opinions and excerpts examined in this chapter bring to light at least four facts of importance to the study of Lydgate: (1) With the end of the eighteenth century, his reputation fell abruptly from that of a great poet to that of a contemptible rhymester. (2) With an occasional exception, neither the early men of letters who admired him as 'the most dulcet sprynge of famous rethoryke'[53] nor the modern critics who despise him as a compiler of 'laureate drivel'[54] have justified their claims with the careful analysis of his poetry; and the latter have at times based their entire verdict upon clearly erroneous assumptions. (3) During the Renaissance, he enjoyed the admiration of men who strongly disapproved of both his religious calling and the subject-matter of some of his works. (4) The charges most commonly brought against him in modern times are those of consistent dullness and prolixity.

Chapter Two

THE OPINIONS RECONSIDERED

THE RADICAL CHANGE OF OPINION toward Lydgate has not passed unnoticed by historians of English literature, and George Ellis was in all likelihood the first to call attention to it. In 1801, at the very time when the scathing criticism of Percy and Ritson was effectively turning into scorn the respect which Lydgate's name had commanded for more than three centuries—and in the same work in which he himself ridiculed the poet's tediousness—Ellis remarked, 'few writers have been more admired by their contemporaries; yet none have been treated with more severity by modern critics'.[1] However, he made no attempt to account for what constituted a minor revolution in literary taste, and he merely concluded, 'Lydgate's popularity was, indeed, excessive and unbounded; and it continued without much diminution during at least, two centuries' (p. 293).

We must return to Lounsbury and the end of the century for an attempt to explain the downfall of Lydgate's reputation. We have seen above that Lounsbury accounted for the poet's early popularity with the argument that his works had appeared at a time when the paucity of English literature did not encourage discrimination. We now find him disqualifying later favourable and even neutral critics:

> I am aware that Lydgate was spoken of respectfully by a man of genius such as Gray, and not disrespectfully spoken of by a

> woman of genius such as was Mrs. Browning. It only proves that, in spite of the dictum of Horace, there are middling verses which the immortals do not despise. Gray, moreover, somewhat like Warton, his successor in these literary investigations, was, to a certain extent, an explorer. Both of them, accordingly, in their comments upon early authors adopted unconsciously the explorer's habit of exaggeration, just as the first voyagers to the New World brought back marvellous stories of fountains of perpetual youth, and El Dorados abounding in gold and silver and precious stones. This will explain, to some extent, the comparatively high estimate they expressed of the production of Lydgate.[2]

Saintsbury has likewise turned his attention to the problem. Although he formulates a more elaborate and scholarly explanation than Lounsbury, he reaches very much the same conclusion. His argument relies on the conviction that former ages enjoyed reading Lydgate simply because they did not know any better: 'Lydgate has not lacked defenders, who would be formidable if their *locus standi* were more certain. The fifteenth century adored him because he combined all its own worst faults, and the sixteenth seems to have accepted him because it had no apparatus for criticism.'[3] To Saintsbury the position of the Elizabethans is plain enough; they liked Lydgate 'simply because they did not understand what was good or bad in Middle English versification' (*ibid.*, p. 228). He further rejects later admirers of Lydgate on the probably correct assumption that they were not well acquainted with the material they were discussing: 'When, after a long eclipse, Lydgate was in two senses taken up by Gray, that poet seems chiefly to have known *The Fall of Princes*, in which, perhaps by dint of long practice, Lydgate's metrical shortcomings are less noticeable than in some other places, and where the dignity and gravity of Boccaccio's Latin has, to some extent, invigorated his style. Warton is curiously guarded in his opinions and a favourable judgment of Coleridge may, possibly, be regarded as very insufficiently based' (*ibid.*).[4] If we recall that Warton considers some of Lydgate's poetry something which Chaucer himself cannot surpass, the presence of the word *guarded* in this statement tempts us to wonder whether Saintsbury was not occasionally as subjective in reading Lydgate criticism as he seems to have been in reading Lydgate himself.

The curious thing about the arguments presented by Lounsbury and Saintsbury is the unflinching self-confidence which they reflect. Neither writer ever questions for an instant the accuracy of his opinion. Thus the task of determining what aspects of Lydgate might prove attractive to one period of history and revolting to another is replaced by the much simpler task of listing general and often quite convincing reasons why the opinions of early English critics were not necessarily valid. We must reach the middle of the twentieth century to find a literary scholar questioning the validity of his own opinions. George Sampson follows Saintsbury in asserting that Lydgate is 'a dull, long-winded and metrically incompetent poet',[5] and he endorses the worst which has been said of that poet when he writes of Ritson's pronouncement, 'each epithet of that summary judgment can be defended' (*ibid.*, p. 84). Yet, he warns us, 'we must not forget that he [Lydgate] was greatly admired by contemporary poets and by successors as late as Hawes and Skelton, and that our first printers produced him largely for a public that evidently wanted him' (*ibid.*, p. 85), and he tactfully concludes his criticism with the admission that 'there may be more in Lydgate than we have yet discovered' (*ibid.*).

The foregoing considerations are by no means intended to show that Lydgate is any better than his reputation. They merely suggest that the contempt in which he is commonly held by modern students of English may be in part a convention accepted by people who have either read very little of his poetry or failed to scrutinize it as objectively as they should. Since the verdicts of Saintsbury and Sampson have appeared respectively in the *Cambridge History of English Literature* and the *Concise Cambridge History of English Literature*, they have almost certainly been influential in guiding the judgment of students of English since the first decade of the twentieth century. Nor must we disregard the influence of Emile Legouis and Louis Cazamian, whose widely read *History of English Literature* soberly asserts that 'with Lydgate decomposition overtook English verse'.[6] Since 1948, and especially in the United States, students are likely to take their cue from Albert C. Baugh, whose *Literary History of*

England[7] they usually commit to memory long before glancing at Lydgate. Unlike many of his predecessors, Baugh always expresses himself with scholarly caution, but he nevertheless confirms the conventional judgment by opening his discussion of Lydgate with a mention of his 'incredibly voluminous writings' (p. 295), by suggesting that 'his standing as a poet would have been higher if he . . . had not made the interminable translations which constitute the great bulk of his writings' (p. 297), and by concluding that 'we should be expecting too much to hope that all his odd jobs should have been done and his extensive commissions executed with the inspiration of high art' (*ibid.*).

The theory which I have advanced here tries to account for some of the contempt in which Lydgate is held by our own age, but it does not explain the criticism of Percy and Ritson. We have seen that, at the time when they wrote, the belief in Lydgate's poetic excellence was as strong and widespread as the present belief in his incompetency. We must assume that they read his works with some care before making bold to reject publicly an opinion which had endured for more than three hundred years and had gathered all the prestige associated with the names of such eminent figures as Warton and Gray. It must be in the course of their reading that they found cause to bring against Lydgate the accusations which have since become commonplace: prolixity and constant dullness. An examination of the validity of these accusations will help us understand something of Lydgate's position in regard to the age in which he wrote.

In reality, the two accusations are one, for prolixity may seem either a virtue or a vice depending on the quality of the writing. To most of us five hundred lines of Shakespeare are wonderful reading, but five hundred lines of the *Poema Morale* would be drudgery. Furthermore, details which are attractive to one age may be repulsive to another. Gray's already-mentioned analogy between Lydgate and Homer suggests an illustration for this point. Since the Homeric poems were composed orally by singers who regulated their narrative according to the reactions of their audience,[8] it follows that the ancient Greeks must have derived some sort of enjoyment from listening to the recitation of the catalogue of ships and leaders in the second book of the *Iliad*; yet, the same passage seems tedious to a majority of modern readers, who do not really care about antique ships and have long ago ceased to respond to whatever emotional appeal the names of Minoan-Mycenaean leaders may have had. Thus, we may agree with Gray and accuse Homer of prolixity in this respect. Conversely, we not uncommonly voice our admiration for the artistry of long but inactive passages in Melville's *Moby Dick* or Proust's *Memories of Things Past*, though another age might possibly consider them deplorable examples of prolixity and dullness. If Lydgate's early readers enjoyed his subject-matter and style, then they may well have considered his voluminousness a virtue rather than a fault. It is even probable that, if Ritson had liked the subject-matter and style, he would have had no complaint about prolixity.

The accusation of dullness is easier to evaluate. No one will deny that there are dull moments in Lydgate, as there may well be in any poet who has produced above 140,000 lines. Yet, even by modern standards, investigation reveals undeniably attractive qualities in his poetry. For the immediate purpose of answering the charge of uniform dullness, it will suffice to examine a few representative passages. The excerpts which follow are intended to suggest that Lydgate, despite whatever shortcomings he may have, ought to be regarded as a competent craftsman occasionally capable of handling his material with the skill of a master.

The most obvious aspect of Lydgate's craftsmanship is probably his ability to express human suffering with such persuasive sympathy as to involve to the utmost the reader's emotions. Consider, for instance, the passage in his *Testament*[9] where the aged monk recalls his decision to take orders: at the age of not quite 15, he saw a wall painting of the Crucifixion with the word *vide* written beside it, along with the injunction 'beholde my mekenesse, O child, and leve thy prede' (746). He immediately obeyed and entered the Benedictine monastery of Bury Saint Edmunds; but only now, as he relives the event in his mind, does he realize the full impact of the tragedy implied in Christ's words, and he reformulates the injunction accordingly:

Behold, O man! lyft up thyn eye and see
What mortall peyne I suffre for thi trespace.
With pietous voys I crye and sey to the:
Beholde my woundes, behold my blody face,
Beholde the rebukes that do me so manace,
Beholde my enemyes that do me so despice,
And how that I to reforme the to grace
Was like a lamb offred in sacryfice. (754–61)

The simplicity of these lines is deeply moving. But let us not be blinded by appearances; this is no accidental simplicity. Rather, it is the result of expert craftsmanship at the service of respectable poetic sensitivity. The parallelism between the concept of 'trespace' in the second line and that of 'reform' in the next to the last line; the concomitant parallelism between man as a sinful onlooker and Christ's redeeming sacrifice; the dramatic shifting of focus, in the fourth, fifth, and sixth lines, from the agents of physical suffering ('woundes') to the sufferer's expression ('face') to the agents of emotional suffering ('rebukes') and finally to the cause of both physical and emotional suffering ('enemyes')—all these are too skilfully organized to be merely the result of accident. The same argument applies to the grammar of the two concluding lines, where the purpose and extent of Christ's sacrifice are emphasized by the shift to an adverbial construction from the previous series of nominal constructions. Likewise, the effectiveness of the vocabulary reveals a highly professional consciousness of poetic language. Within context, such expressions as 'pietous voys', 'my woundes', and 'blody face' evoke with brutal clarity the kind of suffering which the poet wishes his reader to understand. The effect which these lines must have had on the religious audience of the fifteenth century may be inferred from the fact that they were considered worthy of being inscribed on the cornices of the Church of the Holy Trinity at Long Melford.[10]

In its emotional appeal, the passage nearly vies with this more celebrated complaint of Christ to man, in the Old-English *Crist*:

Ic wæs on worulde wædla   þæt ðu wurde welig in heofonum;
earm ic wæs on eðle þinum   þæt þu wurde eadig on minum.[11]

The principle at work in both cases is a familiar one: the

voluntary victim of torment reminds his wilfully passive audience that the sufferings he endures are for their sake. Its use is by no means restricted to the Christian tradition, and we find it operating in such culturally and chronologically distant places as the concluding lines of *Prometheus Bound* and the words which Dickens puts in the mouth of Magwitch, towards the end of *Great Expectations*, when the latter tells the yet ungrateful Pip of the sacrifices he underwent to redeem him from poverty. I do not pretend, of course, to place Lydgate on a level with Aeschylus or the author of *Crist*, but we must grant him the ability to use with some distinction a device associated with recognized masters from widely different times and places.

Among the qualities which Gray found in Lydgate, he mentioned his 'art in raising the more tender emotions of the mind'.[12] A glance at the *Life of Our Lady* will justify this opinion. The lines quoted below are spoken by the Virgin Mary to the Child Jesus immediately after the Nativity. Note the effective use which the poet makes of an oxymoronic situation. The mixed sentiments which the young mother expresses towards the helpless creature who is at the same time her newborn child and her everlasting Lord are carefully worked into an extremely touching scene:

> Lyeth in a stall, of chere moste debonayre,
> Tofore my face, my joye and my comforte,
> Whiche with the lokynge of his iyen faire
> Is hool my gladnesse and fully my disporth,
> Sothefaste pleasaunce and my chefe resorte,
> My dere sonne and my [Lorde] also,
> To who with hert and all that I can do.
>
> I thanke the, Lorde that liggiste me beforne,
> That thou luste chese to have affection
> Of me so mekely in erthe to be borne,
> And fro thy Fadre to descende doune,
> Only for helpe and [the] savacion
> Of all mankynde frely of thy wille.
> My blisset chylde, that so goodly stylle
>
> Liggest nowe here mekely be sufferaunce,
> Amyddeste these bestes, so fayre upon to see,

And hast no wight to thyne attendaunce,
Lyke thyne estate a wayting upon the,
Save that thou haste so goodly chosyn me,
Of thy grace, upon the to abyde—
I to serve and thou to be my guyde. (III, 267–87)[13]

Nor does Lydgate's sensitivity to human emotions reveal itself in Christian hagiography only. The story of Canace and Macareus, in his *Fall of Princes*, is a case in point. It tells how Canace, the daughter of King Eolus, allowed her relationship to her brother Macareus to grow more intimate than social conventions are wont to tolerate. When she gave birth to a beautiful boy, Eolus wasted no time to decree death for both child and parents, but Macareus fled rather than submit to the sentence. The excerpt which follows is from a letter which Canace writes to her brother and lover before killing herself:

Thou were whilom my bliss and al my trust,
Sovereyn confort my sorwes to appese,
Spryng and well off al myn hertis lust;
And now, alas, cheeff roote off my disese.
But yiff my deth myht do the any ese,
O brother myn, in remembraunce off tweyne,
Deth shal to me be plesaunce and no peyne.

Mi cruel fader, most ommerciable,
Ordeyned hath—it needis mut be soo,
In his rigour he is so ontretable,
Al merciles he will that it be doo—
That we algate shal deie bothe too.
But I am glad, sithe it may been noon other,
Thou art escapid, my best beloved brother.

This is myn eende, I may it nat asterte,
O brother myn, there is no mor to seye.
Lowli besechyng with al myn hoole herte
For to remembre, speciali I preie,
Yiff it befall my litil sone deie,
That thou maist afftir sum mynde upon us have,
Suffre us bothe be buried in o grave.

I holde hym streihtli atwen myn armys tweyne;
Thou and Nature leide on me this charge.

He gilteles with me mut suffre peyne;
And sithe thou art at fredam and at large,
Lat kyndenesse our love nat so discharge,
But have a mynde, where-ever that thou be,
Onys a day upon my child and me.

On the and me dependith the trespace
Touchyng our gilte and our gret offence;
But, wellaway, most angelik off face,
Our yonge child in his pur innocence
Shal ageyn riht suffre dethis violence,
Tendre off lymes, God wot, ful gilteles,
The goodli faire that lith heere specheles.

A mouth he hath, but woordis hath he noone,
Cannat compleyne, alas, for non outrage,
Nor gruchith nat, but lith heer al aloone,
Stille as a lamb, most meek off his visage.
What herte off steel coude doon to hym damage
Or suffre hym deie, beholdyng the maneer
And look benygne off his tweyne even cleer? (I, 6896–936)

Here as in the excerpt from the *Life of Our Lady*, the technique is one of paradox: the cause of Canace's sorrow was once the cause of her happiness; her child has a mouth with which to speak, but he is too little to use it. The skill with which Lydgate handles his subject stands out by contrast with an account of the same letter in the *Confessio Amantis*, where John Gower's heavy hand piles up antonym upon antonym:

O thou my sorwe and my gladnesse,
O thou myn hele and my siknesse,
O my wanhope and al my trust,
O my desese and al my lust,
O thou my wele, O thou my wo,
O thou my frend, O thou my fo,
O thou my love, O thou myn hate,
For thee mot I be ded algate.[14]

Whereas the tragedy of Canace in the *Fall of Princes* stirs our deepest sympathies, the corresponding episode in the *Confessio Amantis* at best interests us and at worst amuses us. In reference to the former, Gray has written that Lydgate 'has touched the very heart-springs of compassion with so masterly a hand as to merit a place among the greatest poets'.[15]

Since the *Fall of Princes* is an adaptation of Boccaccio's *De Casibus Virorum Illustrium*, it is of interest that the Latin text makes no mention of Canace; and although we find her in Laurent de Premierfait's French translation of the *De Casibus*, she is there despatched in a few lines without any mention of her letter.[16] There is, of course, no reason to think that Lydgate was unacquainted with Gower's version of the letter, but the *Confessio Amantis* says nothing about the paradox of the death penalty imposed upon an innocent child and devotes only one line to Canace's wish to be buried in the same tomb with him. We may accordingly conclude that Lydgate probably drew his inspiration directly from Ovid's *Heroides*, where both points are developed at some length:

> Quid puer admissit tam paucis editus horis?
> Quo laesit facto uix bene natus auum?
> Si potuit meruisse necem, meruisse putetur,
> A! miser admisso plectitur ille meo.
>
> . . . . .
>
> Tu tamen, o frustra miserae sperate sorori,
> Sparsa, precor, nati collige membra tui
> Et refer ad matrem socioque impone sepulcro,
> Vrnaque nos habeat quamlibet arta duos. (109–26)[17]

Three principal differences between Lydgate and Ovid's treatment of the letter must be noted here. Although the English text is six lines longer than the Latin, it eliminates all the background of the story in order to concentrate upon Canace's sorrow and her immediate predicament; it substitutes her sense of grievous sin for what is in the Latin her despair over a tragic accident (113–15); and it has her write the letter before, rather than after, the death of her child. The addition of the element of sin may be accounted for by the fact that Lydgate was a Christian monk retelling a pagan story, and it may possibly have been prompted by Laurent's statement that 'le roy aussi par ung varlet envoya une espee a sa fille Canaces affin quelle fist de soy ce quelle avoyt desservi mais les hystoriens taisent se elle se occist; toutesfoys Macharaun . . . sentant son horrible peche . . . sen fuyt' (p. 171). The other two changes, however, bear witness to Lydgate's narrative skill. Not bound as was Ovid by the exclusively epistolary scheme of the *Heroides*, he eliminates from the letter all such matters as are not strictly relevant and thus succeeds in making it the emotional centre of the tragic story. The change in the relative timing of the letter is likewise aesthetically significant, for it adds to Canace's sorrow an element of anxiety necessarily absent from the Latin version. No one today would seriously compare Lydgate with Ovid, but we must recognize that examination of his treatment of Canace's letter reveals highly effective narrative devices of which his greater predecessor failed to avail himself.

Lydgate likewise displays competent craftsmanship in his courtly love poetry, the boldness of which occasionally compels our attention. Three stanzas from the *Floure of Curtesy*[18] will bear out my statement. In this poem a lover whose suit is at least temporarily thwarted by conventions has walked into a grove where he beholds a multitude of birds mating to their heart's content, hence his bitter exclamation:

> And whyle that I, in my drery payne,
> Sate and beheld aboute on every tre
> The foules sytte alway twayne and twayne,
> Than thought I thus: 'Alas, what may this be,
> That every foule hath his lyberte
> Frely to chose after his desyre
> Everyche his make thus fro yere to yere?
>
> The sely wrenne, the tytemose also,
> The lytel redbrest have free election
> To flyen yfere and togyther go
> Where as hem lyst, aboute envyron,
> As they of kynde have inclynacion,
> And as Nature, emperesse and gyde
> Of every thyng, lyste to provyde.
>
> But man alone, alas, the harde stounde,
> Ful cruelly by Kyndes ordynaunce
> Constrayned is and by statute bounde,
> And debarred from al suche plesaunce.
> What meneth this! What is this purveyaunce

Of God above agayne al right of kynde,
Without cause, so narowe man to bynde.' (50–70)

We need not dwell upon the obviously erotic nature of the imagery, but we should note the skilful use which the poet makes of it. By emphasizing the violent contrast between the birds' unchecked promiscuity and the stern restrictions imposed upon man, he unequivocally brings home to the reader the poignancy of the lover's frustration. We must further observe the highly effective use of a bold initial half-line to bring out the speaker's revolt against the convention that binds him: 'What meneth this!' The very same device, one recalls, serves a similar purpose in one of Surrey's best-known poems: 'Lord, what abuse is this!'[19] The *Floure of Curtesy* is not a particularly imaginative love complaint, but the quality of its execution makes it a highly reputable specimen of its genre.

Not only does Lydgate know how to write a lover's complaint, but he also knows how to set the physical background for it, as witnessed by the following two stanzas from his *Complaint of the Black Knight*:[20]

And in I went to her the briddes songe,
Which on the braunches, both in pleyn and vale,
So loude songe that al the wode ronge
Lyke as hyt sholde shever in pesis smale
And as me thoughte that the nyghtyngale
Wyth so grete myght her voys gan out wrest
Ryght as her hert for love wolde brest.

The soyle was pleyn, smothe, and wonder softe,
Al oversprad wyth tapites that Nature
Had made herselfe, celured eke alofte
With bowys grene, the floures for to cure,
That in her beaute they may not longe endure
Fro al assaute of Phebus fervent fere,
Which in his spere so hote shone and clere. (43–56)

The general impression is appropriately one of lushness, and it is significant that the imagery seems expressly calculated to appeal most invitingly to the four senses of hearing ('the briddes song'), touch ('soyle . . . wonder softe'), sight ('bowys grene'), and smell ('floures'). The last three lines deserve special notice.

With the term *assaute* the poet introduces an unexpected element of strife into a hitherto harmonious scene. Within context the pun on the sexual overtone of the term is obvious, for *assaute* already had in Lydgate's time the same double meaning which it has today,[21] and only this interpretation can explain the statement that it is the beauty of the flowers that makes it impossible for them to resist Phebus's fervent fire. The stanzas under discussion echo respectively—at times to the very words—those two passages in Chaucer's *Book of the Duchess* where the dreamer thinks himself awakened by a concert of small birds and later follows a dog along a lush, flowery path. Although obviously lacking the humorous and self-amused tone which pervades the Chaucerian passages, Lydgate's strongly sensual and connotative description establishes a particularly adequate setting for the remainder of the poem, during which a lovesick knight will enter the grove to pray Venus for the favours of his beloved.

The extracts considered thus far have been static and largely reflective. By contrast, the episode discussed below is concerned with violent physical action; it comes from the *Siege of Thebes* and relates the Thebans' nocturnal ambush of the Argive hero Tydeus. We note at a glance the impressive picture of the surrounded warrior letting his sword 'glyde' among his assailants:

> And than at onys they upon hym falle
> On every part be compas envyroun.
> But Tydeus thorgh his hegh renoun
> His blody swerde lete about hym glyde,
> Sleth and kylleth upon every side
> In his yre and his mortal tene. (2182–7)

As Tydeus rises to his feet after being unhorsed, the poet uses two similes to make us visualize his desperate valour:

> But of knyghthod and of gret prouesse
> Up he roos maugre all his foon,
> And as they cam he slogh hem oon by on
> Lik a lyoun rampaunt in his rage.
>
> . . . . .
>
> And liche a boor stondyng at his diffence

As his foomen proudly hym assaylle,
Upon the pleyn he made her blode to raylle
Al environ that the soyl wex rede. (2194–2203)

The comparison of a surrounded warrior to a lion and a boar is by no means novel, but the effectiveness of an image depends very little on its novelty and very much on its suitability to the context in which it appears. To an age that considered the lion the bravest and most powerful of all beasts, the image must have proved a powerful evocation of the splendid effort required of Tydeus to rise under the tremendous weight of his armour in order to hold off a horde of murderous but inferior adversaries. As for the effectiveness of the comparison with a boar at bay, we need only recall the second hunting scene in *Sir Gawain and the Green Knight*[22] to visualize the kind of image which Lydgate's description must have evoked for an audience that considered hunting the noblest of all games.

The conclusion of the combat in the *Siege of Thebes* is handled with particular felicity. The picture of Tydeus covered with gore, towering alone while the moonlight bathes the bodies of his enemies fallen about him, assumes a majesty unexpected in a poet whose utter incompetence we have learned to take for granted:

Hymsilf yhurt and ywounded kene,
Thurgh his harneys bledyng on the grene,
The Theban knyghtes in compas rounde aboute
In the vale lay slayen all the route,
Which pitously ageyn the mone gape. (2221–5)

Here Lydgate falls only a little short of these two more famous scenes, in the *Chanson de Roland* and the *Nibelungenlied* respectively, in which Roland surveys his massacred army and Gunther and Hagen stand alone before the great charred hall of King Etzel, proudly waiting for Dietrich himself among the corpses of foes and friends.

The repetition of the term *compas* in the scene under discussion is noteworthy. It serves to describe the position of the Thebans both at the beginning (2184) and at the conclusion of the battle (2223), thus drawing a clear parallel between the pride of their onslaught and the stillness of their death. This method of emphasizing Tydeus's heroism and victory in the face of utterly hopeless odds remains effective to this day; it may have been even more so with the original audience of the poem, for the *Siege of Thebes* was finished only a few years after Agincourt, and Axel Erdmann has argued in his authoritative edition that 'in painting Tydeus' character and extolling his exploits, the author had, no doubt, in his mind's eye England's youthful hero, King Henry V'.[23] If we momentarily return to the two images discussed earlier and consider them in the light of Erdmann's theory, we shall find that they gain a new depth of meaning and a higher level of effectiveness. Every educated man in the fifteenth century had heard of the Great Chain of Being and probably knew that, just as Henry was king of men, the lion was king of beasts: one was nearest God among men, the other nearest to God among beasts. Likewise, almost every Englishman of the time may be assumed to have accepted the perhaps romantic notion that Henry had stood his ground against the French at Agincourt exactly as a boar at bay stands his ground against the hunters who outnumber him. It is significant that Henry Noble MacCracken has rather convincingly argued that the *Siege of Thebes* was intended for Henry's own perusal.[24]

Even if one wishes to exercise caution, the foregoing considerations justify at least the conclusion that Lydgate knew how to suit imagery to context.[25] I am adding a few isolated verses and brief statements in order to illustrate the qualities which a random sampling of his works will reveal. The two lines below, for instance, are probably proverbial, but the question with which they begin a stanza on the fickleness of women has a startling effect somewhat reminiscent of Donne's 'Go and catch a falling star':

> What man may the wind restreyne
> Or holde a snake by the tayle?[26]

The following description of the nightingale's death—a symbol for that of Christ—deserves notice for its metrical felicity and delicacy of sentiment:

> Hir song, hire myrth and melody was done,
> And she expyred aboute the oure of none.[27]

The same may be said of these two verses on the mutability of human affairs:

> The world so wyde, the ayre so remevable
> The sely man so lytell of stature. . . .[28]

Only a very great poet would need apologize for the tone of this invitation of Christ to the soul of man:

> Come to my gardyn and to myn herber grene,
> My fayre suster and my spouse deere.[29]

Such lines as 'Kome on, my frend, my brother most entere',[30] and 'O ruby, rubifyed in the Passyoun',[31] and '. . . the larke song/With notes newe hegh up in the ayr'[32] carry something of their impact beyond the context in which they appear, and are quite typical of their author at his best.

Lydgate, we all know, is not always at his best, and I must emphasize here that I am not arguing the uniform reputability of his production; I am only pleading for the recognition of such virtues as may be found in some of his works. Nor am I arguing that these virtues, real as I believe them to be, are always of the first order. For example, several of the excerpts discussed above suggest that, unlike the majority of recognized masters, Lydgate is not above availing himself to the full of whatever situations may appeal to the reader's sentimentality. Yet, these excerpts have undeniable qualities; and the poems from which they are taken must have been at least in part known to Percy and Ritson, for they were fairly easily obtainable at the turn of the eighteenth and nineteenth century. We have already seen that the *Siege of Thebes* had been issued and reissued by the early English printers; the same is true of the *Life of Our Lady*, the *Floure of Curtesy*, and the *Complaint of the Black Knight.*[33] Among these, the *Floure of Curtesy* and the *Siege of Thebes* must have been considered fairly representative of their author, since Alexander Chalmers included them in the anthology of English poetry which he published in 1810.[34] Nor could Ritson have been unaware of their authorship, since he himself ascribed them to Lydgate.[35]

If we accept my previous argument that Percy and Ritson probably derived their contempt for Lydgate from a careful sampling of his works, we may wonder at their failure to have taken any notice of his very real, though limited, competence. It may be, of course, that they were aware of the qualities which we have noted above, but found them falling so short of the reputation they were about to challenge that they chose to ignore them in favour of equally real weaknesses to which they wanted to draw attention. It may also be that, as D'Israeli believed,[36] Ritson's profound dislike for the monastery was responsible for the gusto with which he set out to discredit the Monk of Bury; and we have no reason to suppose that Percy was anything but out of sympathy with much of the subject-matter in Lydgate. Plausible as these theories sound, however, they are not really convincing, for they imply a basic intellectual dishonesty which one hesitates to impute to the scholars whose views are being discussed here. A more satisfactory explanation is that they searched Lydgate in hope of finding Chaucer, or at least a good imitation of him, and their disappointment at failing to find qualities that were not there led them to overlook qualities that were. This possibility is born out by the abuses which we have already heard Ritson heap upon Lydgate for falling short of Chaucer, and if it is correct it will provide us with at least a partial explanation for the disrepute in which Lydgate has fallen since the beginning of the nineteenth century. The imitator automatically finds himself at an initial disadvantage with the critics: whenever his work resembles that which he has presumably imitated, he can be dismissed as lacking imagination; whenever he comes forth with something original he opens himself to the accusation of having failed in his capacity of imitator.

That Ritson would be disappointed at not finding Chaucer while reading Lydgate may also be inferred from his own statement, when he omitted all mediaeval literature except Chaucer from his own *English Anthology* on the ground that 'the niceties of the present age [were] ill disposed to make the necessary allowances for the uncouth diction and homely sentiments of former ages'.[37] That he and his contemporaries had good reasons to look for Chaucer while reading Lydgate follows both from the earlier practice of comparing the two poets and from Lydgate's own habit of referring to Chaucer as his master.[38]

Despite these references to Chaucer—which, incidentally, are commonplaces with all the principal writers of the time[39]—we may question the advisability of evaluating Lydgate by the same criteria as his great predecessor. Although his metres and many of his works are Chaucerian in form, and although his direct borrowings from Chaucer are far too numerous to be analysed here, a substantial part of his production differs from that of Chaucer not merely in the execution but especially in the intention. Even on the part of less vociferous critics than Ritson, the assumption that Lydgate ought to resemble Chaucer has resulted in many unfounded generalizations, as William J. Courthope's evaluation of the *Siege of Thebes* will illustrate: 'While Chaucer alters, invents, improves, and omits, showing at every touch the working of an independent judgment, Lydgate makes his digest of the *Thebais* in the spirit of a lawyer's clerk, depriving a poem, not very interesting in itself, of its life and character with such success, that his version of the "story" resembles his original in about the same degree as the chronicle of Eutropius resembles the history of Livy.'[40] For the reader unfamiliar with Lydgate's poem, the following information will suggest the extent of the generalization into which Courthope allowed himself to be led by his reluctance to settle for anything less than Chaucer: although scholars had long known that Statius' *Thebaid* was not the original of the *Siege of Thebes*, it was not until nineteen years after the publication of the statement quoted here that Axel Erdmann and Eilert Ekwall finally produced enough evidence to identify the probable source as a French prose romance, of which the English poem is an expansion rather than a digest.[41] Indeed, the whole issue was still in serious doubt until 1961,[42] so that we are entitled to question the validity of Courthope's comparison of the poem to whatever work he calls its 'original'—even if we grant that Chaucer would probably have done a better job than Lydgate.

The determination to find Chaucer in Lydgate has occasionally tricked even the most thorough and authoritative scholars into assertions which ought to have been qualified. For instance, when the expression 'whiche me semyth owghte inow suffice' appears toward the end of the *Serpent of Division*,[43] MacCracken starkly comments, 'a line straight from Chaucer' (p. 71). We know that Chaucer often uses the three-word combination 'owghte inow suffice',[44] and Lydgate may well have thought of him when he wrote the line in question. Chaucer, however, is not the only poet to have used the expression before the fifteenth century,[45] and Joseph Schick assures us that 'this expression, which now appears pleonastic, was very common'.[46] Thus we cannot disregard the possibility that Lydgate may have written his line without giving a thought to Chaucer.

Along with the conviction that Lydgate ought to be evaluated according to the success with which he emulates Chaucer, we not seldom find the assumption that he must be understood as a completely mediaeval poet. We are told, for instance, that he is 'certainly the fullest example we have of the mediaeval mind in poetry',[47] and that 'his masters in opinion and sentiment were the compilers of the "Gesta Romanorum" '.[48]

Although Lydgate exhibits most of the qualities usually associated with the Middle Ages and his debt to Chaucer is admittedly immense, examination of his poetry against the background of the age in which he lived will suggest that the views outlined above are not entirely correct. I shall try to show in the remainder of this study that Lydgate can be best understood, not as a strictly mediaeval Chaucerian, but rather as a poet who immediately followed Chaucer and wrote during the period of transition between the Middle Ages and the Renaissance. The qualification may seem small, but it will allow us to evaluate Lydgate's production according to its own merits instead of condemning him for repeatedly falling short of a goal at which he was not always aiming.

Chapter Three

THE PERIOD OF TRANSITION

BEFORE INVESTIGATING Lydgate's position between the Middle Ages and the Renaissance we must consider briefly the nature of the period of transition between these two eras. So much has already been written on the subject that we need not formulate any new theory or seek new supporting evidence; but the existence of occasionally essential disagreements between some of these theories makes it necessary to select and agree upon certain assumptions which underlie the present study.

Some of the current theories concerning the shift from what we call the Middle Ages to what we call the Renaissance must be rejected here for the practical reason that they almost automatically eliminate the possibility of discussing the period of transition between the two. To mention only the most extreme positions, some scholars like to think that the Renaissance burst out in all its glory and made a clean sweep of the Middle Ages the instant that Petrarch set pen to ink to compose his letter to Cicero, while others seem to believe that there simply was no Renaissance at all. On the one hand Erwin Panofsky argues that 'something fairly decisive . . . must have happened . . . during the fifteenth century. . . . The historian of art and literature, at least, will have to admit the reality of . . . a Renaissance which, with surprising impetus, superseded a period of utter non-classicality.'[1] On the other hand Johan Nordström asserts that 'what we have learned to think of as the great contributions of the Renaissance to western culture appears more and more . . . a simple continuation or transformation of the Middle Ages'.[2] Depending on the point of view, either theory may be right or wrong.

The most obvious weakness of the argument in favour of a sudden Renaissance is that it goes against common sense. The division of history into specific chronological periods is almost necessarily an arbitrary device established for the convenience of scholars. Short of a cataclysm, cultural changes do not occur on a specific date. We can, of course, say that Byzantine culture underwent a radical change on May 29, 1453, because of the Turkish sack of Byzantium;[3] but we cannot say that the Romantic period ended and the Victorian period began with Dickens's publication of *Pickwick Papers* in 1836–7, even though students of literature may find it convenient to do so for scholarly and pedagogical reasons. In respect to the Middle Ages and the Renaissance, Johan Huizinga has stated the case with utmost clarity:

> The transition from the spirit of the declining Middle Ages to humanism was far less simple than we are inclined to imagine it. Accustomed to oppose humanism to the Middle Ages, we would gladly believe that it was necessary to give up the one in order to embrace the other. We find it difficult to fancy the mind cultivating the ancient forms of medieval thought and expression while aspiring at the same time to antique wisdom and beauty. Yet this is just what we have to picture to ourselves. Classicism did not come as a sudden revelation, it grew up among the luxuriant vegetation of medieval thought. Humanism was a form before it was an inspiration. On the other hand, the characteristic mode of thought of the Middle Ages did not die out till long after the Renaissance.[4]

The most obvious weakness of the argument against a Renaissance is that it goes squarely against the testimony of the people who lived during the period which we have been used to call by that name. Rightly or wrongly, the intellectuals of the Renaissance seem to have been convinced that a wide chasm separated them from their ancestors and that their own age had ushered in a rebirth of art and learning. For instance, Filippo

Villani, writing in Florence at the end of the fourteenth century, assures us that there was not a decent poem composed since the death of Claudian until Dante brought poetry back from the 'shadows into light' nine hundred years later. About 1525 we find Albrecht Dürer already using the term *Wiedererwachsung*, and in 1550 we hear Giorgio Vasari discuss what he calls the *rinascità* of the arts.[5] Joseph Bédier and Paul Hazard have reminded us that the writers of the Renaissance referred to their own time as the 'retour de l'âge d'or', the 'lumière dissipant les ténèbres gothiques et les brumes cimmériennes', and the 'restitution des bonnes lettres', and that 'Amyot rappelle à Henry II que François I avait "heureusement fondé et commencé de faire *renaistre* et florir . . . les bonnes lettres" '.[6] C. S. Lewis makes light of this kind of evidence;[7] but, as Howard E. Hugo has shown about the Romantics, there are at least some reasons for thinking that the self-awareness of a cultural movement may be one of the cues to the actual existence of that movement.[8] Be this as it may, we find the sentiments discussed here clearly expressed during the later Renaissance in the famous praise of François Villon included in Boileau's *Art Poétique*:

> Villon sut le premier dans ces siècles grossiers
> Debrouiller l'art confus de nos vieux romanciers.[9]

Even admitting the principle of a Renaissance, however, we may wonder whether it came about with such a sudden impetus as some of its advocates would have us believe. I am not denying that the impetus was there; I am only suggesting that it may have come as the result of a period of transition during which the mediaeval and Renaissance elements discussed by Huizinga were possibly mixed in more equal proportions than either before or after. On this point Bédier and Hazard, who emphasize the difference between the two periods, warn us that the ideals of the Renaissance did not suddenly come into being, but that the way had been paved for them 'par des efforts confus' of the immediately preceding era.[10]

Transitions tend to blur distinctions between even the most radical opposites. Whether or not we like the sentiment, we must agree with the fact in Ogden Nash's statement, 'The trouble with a kitten is that/Eventually it becomes a cat.' Yet very few of us could tell the exact moment when the kitten becomes the cat. Rather, we go on assuming that we have a kitten in the house until, one fine day, some insignificant incident makes us realize that the kitten is in reality a cat and has been so for several weeks. We never noticed the change because it took place over a period of transition during which the characteristics of the kitten blended with those of the cat. Students of the English language know that the same thing is true of the change from Old English to Middle English. The Middle English of Chaucer and the Old English of the *Beowulf* poet are almost as different as, say, French and Latin. Yet the change did not take place suddenly and the compilers of the *Anglo-Saxon Chronicle* did not immediately shift from Old English to Middle English upon hearing of William's victory at Hastings. In certain respects it is difficult to tell the difference between texts written some hundred years before the Conquest and texts written thirty years after it.[11]

The same principle applies to the Middle Ages and the Renaissance, at least as they have manifested themselves in the literature of England. Everyone takes for granted that Chapman's translation of Homer is in the spirit of the Renaissance and that the *Ormulum* is in the spirit of the Middle Ages, but we find it much harder to make similar distinctions between works written during the fifteenth century. Here, however, we must take another phenomenon into account: precisely because they tend to be noticed belatedly, the slowest changes often appear sudden and surprising. The point may be illustrated by the juxtaposition of Chaucer and the Scottish poet Gavin Douglas, who wrote respectively immediately before the beginning and immediately after the end of the fifteenth century.

Despite occasional attempts at making Chaucer a harbinger of the Renaissance, most students of English look upon him as a thoroughly mediaeval poet. Indeed, C. S. Lewis has argued that the adaptation of Boccaccio's *Filostrato* into *Troilus and Criseyde* was in part the transformation of 'a Renaissance story into a medieval story'.[12] This opinion was expressed in 1936, and it is still up to date with Chaucerian scholars in the second half of the twentieth century, as Charles Muscatine makes clear with the acknowledgment that 'C. S. Lewis is the first critic to have grasped the historical significance of what Chaucer did to *Il Filostrato*.[13] Even E. M. W. Tillyard, who expresses serious reservations about Lewis's claim, must turn to Chaucer for 'typically medieval figures'.[14] Nor is Chaucer an exception to his age. A roll call of the great works of the period would sound like a check-list of the mediaeval masterpieces of English literature: *Sir Gawain and the Green Knight*, *Pearl*, *Piers Plowman*, the *Parliament of the Three Ages*, and the like.

In contrast to Chaucer, we may look upon Gavin Douglas as the author of one of the signposts of the early English Renaissance. His *Eneados*, composed thirteen years after the close of the fifteenth century, is the first translation of Virgil's *Aeneid* into English. Even C. S. Lewis, who would place it 'in the mediaeval tradition',[15] admits its being decidedly closer to the Latin text than Dryden's translation.[16] If we have any doubt about the spirit in which the work was done, we need only read the section of the introduction where Douglas discusses the immediate predecessor of his own poem, Caxton's translation from the French of the typically mediaeval *Roman de Eneas*:

> . . . William Caxtoun, of Inglis nation,
> In pross hes prent ane buik of Inglis gros,
> Clepand it Virgill in *Eneados*—
> Quilk that he sais of Frensch he did translait.
> It hes nathing ado therwith, God wait,
> Nor na mair like than the devill and Sanct Austyne:
> Have he no thank therfor, bot lost his pyne!
> So schamfully that storye did pervert,
> I red his werk with harmes at my hert
> That sic ane buik, but sentence or engyne,
> Suld be intitillit efter the poet divyne.
> His ornait goldin versis, mair than gilt,
> I spittit for despyt to see sua spilt
> With sic a wycht, quhilk treulie, be myne entent,
> Knew never thre wowrdis of all that Virgill meant.[17]

Douglas's indictment of Caxton is as clear as it is vigorous: it reproaches him with having betrayed the lesson and diction of a classical author, that is to say, with having done precisely the thing which seemed most natural to the mediaeval mind, as witnessed by *Ovide Moralisé*, the *Roman de Troy*, the *Alexanderlied*, the *Lay of Sir Orfeo*, and countless others.

Whereas Caxton's text follows the mediaeval French *Roman de Eneas*, the goal which Douglas sets for himself is the accurate rendition into English of both the text and the spirit of Virgil's poem. The attempt is in keeping with the spirit which Panofsky considers symptomatic of the Renaissance, and it is so successful that the *Eneados* remains in many respects the truest translation of the *Aeneid* in the English language. In particular, it succeeds in rendering the vitality which pervades so many scenes of action in the Latin. Consider, for instance, the passage where Venus shows Aeneas the destruction of Troy:

> hic, ubi disjectas moles avulsaque saxis
> saxa vides, mixtoque undantem pulvere fumum,
> Neptunus muros magnoque emota tridenti
> fundamenta quatit totamque a sedibus urbem
> eruit. Hic Juno Scaeas saevissima portas
> prima tenet sociumque furens a navibus agmen
> ferro accincta vocat.[18]

The impression conveyed by these lines is one of cataclysmic action, and the Scottish text evokes precisely the same thing:

> Quhar thir towris thou seis doun fall and sweye,
> And stane fra stane doun bet, and reik wprise,
> With stew, puldir, and dust mixt on this wise,
> Neptune the fundmentis of thir wallis hie,
> With his greit matok havand granis thre,
> Wndermyndis rond about the towne,
> Furth of the ground holkand the barmkin doune.
> Maist cruel Juno has, or this, alswa
> Sesit with the first the port clepit Sceya,
> And from the schippis the ostis in sche callis,
> Standand wode wraithe enarmyt on the wallis. (II, 106)

It is true that Douglas does not translate Virgil word for word, but the expressions which he uses render accurately the spirit of their Latin counterparts as well as the visual images therein, while avoiding the awkwardness of the specific English equivalents. For instance, translating *moles* by its nearest equivalent, *large structures*, would result in a double betrayal of Virgil, for the

English expression is entirely lifeless and evokes at best a very imprecise image. *Towris*, on the contrary, has all the force and visual value which the Latin term has within context, especially if we keep in mind that Douglas's audience must have assumed Troy to look like a fortified city of the early sixteenth century.

Later translators have been less fortunate in their attempts. Dryden, for instance, renders the first line as 'Where yon disorder'd heap of ruin lies',[19] thus missing the immediate sense of action, the specificity of the image, and the awesome magnitude of the scene suggested by both Virgil and Douglas. C. Day Lewis takes all the life out of the line when he translates it, 'Now, look at/That litter of masonry there . . .',[20] and J. W. Mackail does very much the same thing with 'here, where thou seest sundered piles of masonry . . .'.[21]

Douglas's respect for the lesson of the pagan whom he is translating clearly reveals the difference between him and the mediaeval poets who dealt with Greece and Rome. His willingness to accept classical antiquity as he finds it is especially noticeable in his treatment of the classical gods. Jean Seznec has shown that the gods were never forgotten during the Middle Ages;[22] but they were either thoroughly domesticated or presented as unequivocal embodiments of the devil. Perhaps because of his episcopal calling, Douglas feels the need of apologizing to his Christian audience for translating things which he says Caxton has labelled 'fenyeit and nocht for to belief' (II, 9), but he shows no intention of either omitting or altering Virgil's treatment of the gods: 'I thame write furth followand his vers' (*ibid.*). His justification for rendering everything as he finds it is simply that 'Virgill therin a hie philosophour him shew' (*ibid.*); and, although he recognizes the theological errors of the Ancients, he warns us, 'All is not fals, traste wele, in caice thai fene' (*ibid.*).

Compare these statements with their counterparts in the prologue to the *Gest Hystoriale of the Destruction of Troy*, which a contemporary of Chaucer adapted rather freely from Guido delle Colonne's *Historia Destructionis Trojae*:

> Now of Troy for to telle is myn entent evyn
>
> . . . . .
>
> But sum poyetis full prist that put hom therto

With fablis and falshed fayned there speche,
And made more of that mater than hom maister were.
Sum lokyt over little, and lympit of the sothe.
Amonges that menye, to myn hym be nome,
Homer was holden haithill of dedis
Qwiles his dayes enduret, derrist of other,
That with the Grekys was gret, and of Grice comyn.
He feynet myche fals was never before wroght,
And traiet the truth, trust ye non other.
Of his trifuls to telle I have no tome nowe,
Ne of his feynit fare that he fore with:
How goddes foght in the filde, folke as thai were,
And other errours unable, that after were knowen,
That poyetis of prise have prevyt untrew.[23]

Whereas Douglas will relate everything in Virgil 'followand his vers', the author of the *Gest* has no time to waste on the 'trifuls' of Homer. By the contrast between these two sentiments we may measure the distance which separates the *Eneados* from an attitude commonly associated with the Middle Ages. Of course, it would be gross exaggeration to describe Douglas as a thorough-going humanist, and we know that Polydore Virgil was very much amused by his faith in mediaeval chronicles in preference to the testimonies of Caesar, Tacitus, and Pliny about the history of Scotland.[24] Yet the respect for the Ancients and their theology which we find expressed in the *Eneados* marks a small but definite step in the direction of a Renaissance attitude best expressed by Joachim Du Bellay: 'Rome fut tout le monde, et tout le monde est Rome.'[25]

Considered out of context, the *Eneados* does not fully bear out my initial claim that it may be considered indicative of the Renaissance, for Renaissance humanism not merely respected and translated Classical Antiquity but reflected its pervasive influence. The *Cambridge History of English Literature* is quite definite and, I believe, quite correct on this point: 'That influence of the Classics on the humanists must not be confounded with the study and translation of Classical authors. . . .'[26] One may likewise point out that an isolated instance is not enough to prove a point. John of Salisbury, perhaps as a result of his Classical studies at Chartres, has often been considered a humanist; yet we do not normally look upon England in the twelfth century as a centre for humanistic studies. Panofsky has convincingly argued that the strong Classical influence noticeable in the *Schatzkammer Gospels* and certain statues in the Cathedral of Rheims by no means justifies giving the name of Renaissance to the periods during which they were produced.[27] In contrast with these examples, the *Eneados* is anything but an isolated phenomenon. On the contrary it should be considered the literary expression of an age of philosophical, historical, and linguistic humanism. It was composed two years after Erasmus's *Praise of Folly*—which was written in England—and the same year with Thomas More's *History of King Richard III* and William Lyly's Latin grammar. Give or take a few years, it is roughly contemporary with William Grocyn's most active period, with Thomas Linacre's *Rudimenta Grammatica*, with John Colet's grammatical treatises, with More's *Utopia*, and with Skelton's *Magnificence*. Looking at the *Eneados* within this context, we are tempted to say that with it the literature of the British Isles was in process of catching up with the Continental Renaissance. The poem was finished the same year with Machiavelli's *Prince*, two years before the final volume of Aldus Manutius's first edition of the Greek authors, only three years before Ariosto's *Orlando Furioso*, fifteen years before Castiglione's *Courtier*, and nineteen years before the first book of Rabelais's *Pantagruel*.

Despite this apparent outburst of humanism, however, the attitudes which we usually associate with the English Renaissance did not suddenly appear with the beginning of the sixteenth century, nor did the writers of that time immediately shake off all vestiges of mediaevalism. It is no accident, for instance, that Walter Schirmer begins his study of English humanism with Duke Humphrey of Gloucester,[28] while the *Cambridge History of English Literature* classifies both Douglas and Skelton under the heading of 'Chaucerians'—along with the thoroughly mediaeval Thomas Hoccleve and the anonymous author of the *Flower and the Leaf*. The scholarly investigation of this paradox lies outside the scope of the present study. We may surmise, however, that the seeds of the Renaissance, which had been imported from Italy by Chaucer and his contemporaries, germinated and grew slowly during the fifteenth century. It is not impossible that by the beginning of the sixteenth century they had so multiplied that the writers of England awoke to the fact and began acting accordingly, thus giving the appearance of a sudden outburst to what may have been only the intensification, however powerful, of a change in intellectual atmosphere which had been taking place with ever-increasing rapidity over the preceding hundred years. We must not forget that human beings almost always act according to their own images of themselves. Like the cat in Ogden Nash's poem, a boy grows progressively into a man, but he begins *acting* like a man very suddenly the day he *realizes* that he is one. The same thing, I believe, is true of nations: as the lesson of history has suggested only too often, they act according to the way they see themselves, hence my suggestion that the writers of England began acting wholeheartedly like humanists the day they realized they were humanists. Not all of them, however, were equally affected by the change, so that only a year before the completion of *The Praise of Folly*, we find Stephen Hawes including purely mediaeval fabliaux in his *Pastime of Pleasure*.

The first Renaissance humanist to visit England was the Florentine Poggio Bracciolini, who arrived in 1418. We know that he was disappointed at the dimness of humanistic knowledge and the rarity of classical texts in England,[29] and he subsequently showed a telling eagerness to avoid returning.[30] Yet, the fact that Poggio's visit was in response to the invitation of Henry Beaufort, Bishop of Winchester, suggests that at least one influential Englishman was interested in the activities of the humanists. Roberto Weiss has shown that Richard Petworth, Beaufort's secretary, was already attracted to the Italian Renaissance several years before Poggio's arrival.[31]

Nor must Poggio's dismay at the inadequacy of English libraries lead us to think that there were no classical texts in England. On the contrary, the library of Bury Saint Edmunds, Lydgate's own monastery, owned an impressive collection of classical texts: Plautus, Terence, Horace, Juvenal, Persius, Virgil, Statius, Seneca, Cicero, Macrobius, Caesar, Sallust, Valerius Maximus, Quintilian, Martianus Capella, Pliny, Dioscorides, Servius, Justin, Aethicus, Solinus, and Vitruvius.[32] H. S. Bennett has quite accurately pointed out that 'Bury . . .

was exceptionally rich with a library of more than 2,000 volumes of sacred and profane literature'.[33] In fact, that library was among the richest of its time, both in England and on the Continent. Considering only accounts from the fourteenth and fifteenth centuries, we find that the library of Christ Church at Canterbury counted 690 volumes; Saint Paul's Cathedral owned 171, Exeter 230, and Merton College, Oxford 1,964. On the Continent, the Louvre Library had 916 volumes, Strassburg Minster 21, Gnessen 35, Hildesheim Cathedral 21 without counting an uncertain number of liturgical works, and Frauenberg 160. The Cathedral collection in Constance, where Poggio first met Henry Beaufort, owned only 200 books according to an inventory dated twenty-five years after that meeting.[34]

Poggio's visit is usually assumed to have had almost no influence on English letters. The assumption is probably correct; yet English humanism seems to have progressed rapidly enough to make the visits of later Italians somewhat less disappointing. A little before the middle of the century Piero del Monte could feel sure enough of his audience to deliver before Henry VI and his Council an oration in quasi-classical Latin and to dedicate to Humphrey of Gloucester a Latin dialogue filled with classical quotations.[35] The works of Thomas Walsingham and John Whethamstede make it difficult to gainsay that humanism and classical studies gained their first foothold among English scholars during the first half of the fifteenth century.[36] From this point on we hear of English men of letters—William Grey, Robert Flemmyng, John Free, John Gunthorpe—travelling to Italy in pursuit of classical learning. Among these, Flemmyng was the first-known fifteenth-century Englishman to learn Greek, and beginning in 1465 he donated to Lincoln College at Oxford his superb collection of Greek and Latin authors.[37] By the last quarter of the fifteenth century the humanistic revolution was well on its way, and the presses at Oxford were turning out the works of the Italian Renaissance and Classical Antiquity for a new lettered public that evidently demanded them.

Possibly the most important single man in the history of early English humanism was Humphrey of Gloucester. Although his tastes must have remained mediaeval enough to convince Hoccleve that he would be pleased by an English version of a tale from the *Gesta Romanorum*, a biographer has written, 'in Humphrey the Renaissance was manifested in its first youth . . . he led the van of the army which set out to conquer the realms of knowledge. . . . In no other Englishman of the time do we find the same love of the ancient classics which characterised Gloucester.'[38] Because he was the son of Henry IV and the brother of Henry V, Humphrey wielded a powerful influence over the opinions of his contemporaries, and he placed that influence at the service of humane letters: as a patron of the new learning, he brought to England such humanists as Tito Livio Frulovisi and Antonio Beccaria; as a lover of literature and philosophy, he commissioned such works as Leonardo Bruni's Latin translation of Aristotle's *Politics* and Pier Candido Decembrio's translation of Plato's *Republic*; as a bibliophile, he accumulated an immense and splendid collection of classical and vernacular masters. His immediate importance to us is that he was Lydgate's most lasting patron. In particular, it was at his request that the poet produced the English version of Boccaccio's *De Casibus Virorum Illustrium.*

We have no proof that Lydgate ever met any of the humanists mentioned above. Yet, considering that he lived the last thirty years of his productive life during the period which saw the birth of humanism in England and that he was in the patronage of an active supporter of the new movement, we may expect to find in his poetry some reflection of the changes which were taking place around him.[39] I have already discussed Saintsbury's contemptuous remark that the fifteenth century adored him because he combined all its worst faults. If Lydgate was as representative of his age as the statement implies, then we may further expect to find the lessons of the humanists increasingly detectable in his later secular works.

Because Lydgate was born thirty years before Chaucer's death, his literary formation necessarily took place at a time when the young poets of England looked up to their great contemporary for a model. Like Usk, Scogan, Walton, Hoccleve, James I of Scotland, Bokenam, and innumerable others,[40] he never ceased praising the master, so that we find one or more references and acknowledgments to Chaucer in seventeen of Lydgate's works written over a period of forty-four years.[41] Accordingly, we need not be surprised to hear him refer to Chaucer as his master in the *Churl and the Bird*, composed about 1400: the *Churl and the Bird* is a poem in which scholars have indeed detected a strong Chaucerian influence; it retells a tale from this most mediaeval of all compilations, the *Gesta Romanorum*; and the works whose immediate influence it reflects—the French fabliaux, the *Disciplina Clericalis*, and Guido delle Colonne's *Historia*—read like so many samples of the mediaeval mind in literature.[42]

It is interesting, however, to find him still referring to Chaucer as his master some thirty-eight or thirty-nine years later, in the *Fall of Princes*. Although the poem occasionally reveals the influence of Chaucer,[43] its author sets out to do precisely what Chaucer did *not* do in the *Monk's Tale*. The two works relate approximately the same stories, but here the similarity ends. Chaucer's general plan comes from the *Romance of the Rose*, and the biographies he takes from Boccaccio's *De Casibus Virorum Illustrium* and *De Claris Mulieribus* are reduced in size and lesson to the barest outlines designed to illustrate the mediaeval concept of tragedy; the principal influences we may detect therein are those of Vincent de Beauvais's *Speculum Historiale* and of Guyart Desmoulins's *Bible Historiale*.[44] Lydgate, on the other hand, takes both his overall scheme and his materials from the *De Casibus*, which he knew in Laurent de Premierfait's French translation; he not only retains Boccaccio's lesson, but we shall see later that he occasionally adds to it in a spirit which may be considered a precursor of the English Renaissance.[45] Thus, if we arbitrarily consider only the *Churl and the Bird* and the *Fall of Princes*, we are tempted to say that between 1400 and 1439 Lydgate travelled intellectually away from the Middle Ages toward the Renaissance while possibly remaining unaware of the change.

To take four important aspects in which the Renaissance is commonly supposed to have differed from the Middle Ages, we may say that it showed enthusiastic approbation for classical antiquity, a passionate belief in the intrinsic dignity of man, a sharp sense of nationalism, and an active concern for the conduct of princes, including the practice of courtesy.[46] In respect to all these investigation will lead us to modify the usual picture of Lydgate as a strictly mediaeval poet, and it will suggest the presence of increasingly noticeable Renaissance elements in his secular poetry toward the end of his literary career.

Chapter Four

THE MEDIAEVAL TRADITION

THAT LYDGATE began his literary career as a Chaucerian and turned out the kind of poetry which we associate with the Middle Ages is undeniable. His first important poem, the *Complaint of the Black Knight*, is illustrative in this respect. In ninety-six rhyme-royal stanzas and an eight-line envoy, the narrator relates how insomnia prompts him to leave his bed and walk to a luxuriant grove where birds of all kinds are singing and selecting their mates. There, within an arbor, he finds a knight dressed in black abandoning himself to the deepest sorrow because his faithful services have done nothing to advance his cause with his beloved. As soon as the knight has finished his complaint and walked away the narrator begins recording his words as he heard them and falls on his knees to pray Venus to have mercy on all lovers.

The frame of the poem is clearly that of Chaucer's *Book of the Duchess*.[1] The cause of the knight's sorrow is different, and the structure is greatly simplified by the elimination of the story of Ceyx and Alcyone, which in Chaucer leads to the conventional dream vision within which the narration takes place; yet both poems have the same characteristic features of a speaker who suffers from insomnia, who goes to the woods, and who hears the complaint of a knight dressed in black. As already suggested in Chapter Two, consideration of individual details in both poems brings out further similarities. Upon entering the woods, for instance, Lydgate finds the birds singing so loudly 'that al the wode rong' (45); likewise, within the frame of his dream, Chaucer is awakened by birds singing so loudly that 'al his chambre gan to rynge' (312). The soil over which Lydgate treads is 'pleyn, smothe, and wonder softe' (50), covered with lush grass, and decked with flowers; in a similar fashion Chaucer describes the place where he stands as 'ful thikke of gras, ful softe and swete,/With floures fele' (399–400). In both poems, the discovery of the sorrowing black knight comes as a surprise and is expressed in similar terms: Lydgate writes 'As I was war, I sawe ther lay a man/In blake' (130–1), and Chaucer 'I was war of a man in blak' (445). Both knights are exceptionally handsome; Chaucer's is a 'wonder wel-farynge knyght' (452) and Lydgate's 'was in sothe, without excepcioun,/To speke of manhod oon the best on lyve' (157–8).

Not only does Lydgate look to the *Book of the Duchess* for the general frame and spirit of his poem, as well as for many of the details, but he also borrows heavily from other works of Chaucer's. Scholars have demonstrated that he has used an entire passage from Fragment A of the *Romaunt of the Rose*,[2] has drawn to a lesser extent on Fragment B,[3] and has taken occasional ideas from the *Knight's Tale*, the *Legend of Good Women*, and *Troilus and Criseyde*.[4]

The influence of the *Troilus* on the *Black Knight* is perhaps more direct and somewhat stronger than has been realized thus far. As Lydgate writes about unhappy love, it is only normal that he should turn for inspiration to the greatest poem on the subject. Chaucer, one recalls, opens his tale with an invocation to Thesiphone under the form of an argument for consonance between mood and subject-matter; he then goes on to assure his audience of his own total ignorance of the ways of love:

> To the clepe I, thow goddesse of torment,
> Thow cruwel Furie, sorwynge evere yn peyne,
> Help me, that am the sorwful instrument,
> That helpeth loveres, as I kan, to pleyne.
> For wel sit it, the sothe for to seyne,
> A woful wight to han a dreny feere,
> And to a sorwful tale, a sory chere.

For I, that God of Loves servantz serve,
Ne dar to Love, for myn unliklynesse,
Preyen for speed. . . . (I, 8–17)

Throughout the poem, he insists that he writes 'of no sentement' (II, 13) and speaks 'of love unfelyngly' (II, 19) because a 'blynd man kan nat juggen wel in hewis' (II, 21). These are the very sentiments with which Lydgate introduces the lover's complaint in the *Black Knight*:

But who shal helpe me now to complayn?
Or who shal now my stile guy or lede?
O Nyobe! let now thi teres reyn
Into my penne, and eke helpe in this nede
Thou woful Mirre, that felist my herte blede
Of pitouse wo, and my honde eke quake,
When that I write for this mannys sake.

For unto wo acordeth compleynyng,
And delful chere unto hevynesse,
To sorow also sighing and wepyng,
And pitouse morenyng unto drerynesse,
And who that shal writen of distresse,
In partye nedeth to knowe felyngly
Cause and rote of al such malady.

But I, alas, that am of wytte but dulle
And have no knowyng of suche mater. . . . (176–91)

In the reference to the 'pitous wo' which overtakes the poet as he writes, one may even venture to hear an echo of Chaucer's magnificent lines in the opening stanza of the *Troilus*:

Thesiphone, thow help me for t'endite
Thise woful vers, that wepen as I write. (I, 6–7)

The same argument holds true in respect to the behaviour of the Black Knight himself. The symptoms of love which he describes in his own complaint are identical in kind and similar in wording to those which Chaucer has Troilus describe in the first *Canticus Troili*. Troilus complains, 'For hete of cold, for cold of hete, I dye' (I, 420),[5] and the Black Knight merely elaborates on the same motif:

With hote and colde my acces ys so meynt,
That now I shyver for defaute of hete,
And hote as glede now sodenly I suete.
Now hote as fire, now colde as asshes dede,
Now hote for colde, now colde for hete ageyn,
Now colde as ise, now as coles rede
For hete I bren. . . . (229–35)

Likewise, the reactions which Chaucer and Lydgate respectively attribute to the lovers in their poems are quite similar. Troilus no sooner discovers that he is in love than he rushes to his bed (I, 359); in the forest the Black Knight has no bed at his disposal, but the lack of appropriate equipment does not deter him from imitating Troilus by throwing himself on the ground to express his emotion (130).

Students of the *Complaint of the Black Knight* have detected many further Chaucerian elements therein,[6] and something of its overall quality may possibly be inferred from the fact that it was at one time ascribed to Chaucer.[7] The poem is not only in the Chaucerian manner, but it is unequivocally in the mediaeval tradition of courtly love. The convention of the whimsical and unattainable woman, which is the cause of the lover's sorrow, is implicit in his exclamation, 'I me compleyn/That she hath joy to laughen at my peyn' (447–8). The convention of the abject lover is illustrated in his reaction to her haughtiness:

And thus I am for my trouthe, alas!
Mordred and slayn with wordis sharp and kene,
Gilteles, God wote, of al trespas,
And lye and blede upon this colde grene.
Now mercie, suete! mercye, my lyves quene!
And to youre grace of mercie yet I prey
In your servise that your man may dey.

. . . . .

I axe mercie in al my best entent,
Redy to dye yf that ye assent.

. . . . .

Sufficeth me to dye in your servise. (512–39)

Within a few lines, we are presented with all the principal figures of the mediaeval allegory of love—Daunger, Dysdeyne, Pite (Routhe, Mercie), and Dispite (497–510). To be sure,

Lydgate shares these features with Chaucer, but he also shares them with the courtly poets of the thirteenth and fourteenth century on the Continent. It is significant that, despite the glaring and multiple borrowings discussed above, his immediate model was probably not a poem by Chaucer but more likely Jehan Froissart's *Dit du Bleu Chevalier*.[8]

Similar arguments may be formulated about most of Lydgate's early pieces. His *Isopes Fabules*, for example, are in the favourite mediaeval tradition of the animal fable[9] and may reflect the influence of Marie de France;[10] his *Flour of Curtesy* is entirely in the tradition of courtly love[11] and owes something to Chaucer's *Parliament of Fowls*;[12] and his *Gentlewoman's Lament* is believed to have taken its form and tone from Chaucer's *Anelida and Arcite* and the French school of love complaints.[13] We have seen in the preceding chapter that *The Churl and the Bird* is likewise a typically mediaeval poem.

Nor did Lydgate discard Chaucer and the French tradition the day he discovered humanism. His *Temple of Glas*, written possibly as late as 1420,[14] is revealing in this respect. Some literary historians have seen in it the influence of Virgil[15] and argued that it is a precursor of Spenser's Panthea, in the second book of *The Faerie Queen*.[16] Correct as these observations certainly are, the *Temple of Glas* reads nevertheless like an imitation of Chaucer's *House of Fame*,[17] and other literary historians have seen in it the influence of the *Romaunt of the Rose*, and Guillaume de Machaut compared it with the romances of Chrestien de Troyes, argued its relationship to the *Squire's Tale*, and offered it as evidence of the vitality of mediaeval courtly love during the first half of the fifteenth century.[18] The truth is that the form and intention of the poem belong to the mediaeval tradition while the execution seems on occasion to reflect something of the new humanism, and the result reads like a mixture of both.[19] I would not be understood to argue that Lydgate ever came into actual contact with Poggio Bracciolini, or even that he was consciously influenced by the doctrines of the humanists at the time when he wrote the *Temple of Glas*. We know, however, that he was intimate with Chaucer's son Thomas,[20] who was himself a friend of that same Henry Beaufort who had invited Poggio to England.[21] Under the circumstances, it seems by no means impossible that Lydgate had at least heard something of the Italian visitor. More important, however, is the fact that he belonged to the circle of a friend of the man who had brought Poggio to England and that it was possibly in this circle that he made the acquaintance of Humphrey of Gloucester,[22] his lasting patron as well as a patron of the new learning. If anything at all of the humanistic doctrines was to filter into English poetry at this early date, then we should logically expect to find the results in Lydgate, since the people for whose friendship he obviously cared and those whose patronage he must have sought were in the vanguard of new movement.

With the passage of the years, we shall see Lydgate partially turn away from Chaucer and the Middle Ages and look toward the Renaissance. In one respect, however, he remains completely mediaeval to the very end: no matter how typical of the Renaissance his lesson may be, the literary conventions to which it subscribes in expressing it come directly from the dicta of mediaeval rhetoric.

Probably the two mediaeval literary conventions which seem most surprising to the modern mind are the denial of authorship, found especially in narrative poems, and the use of the so-called topos of affected modesty, whereby the poet insists upon his own feebleness and inadequate preparation.[23] Ever since the Renaissance we have grown accustomed to finding poets eager to claim the authorship of their production and ready to assert its everlasting beauty. We recall how Ronsard in *Sonnet VI* assures his coy mistress that no one will take notice of her after old age has shrivelled her skin and thinned her hair; but, should she happen to mutter, 'Ronsard me celebroit du temps que j'estois belle',[24] then even the lowliest servant will suddenly awaken to praise her name:

> Lors vous n'aurez servante oyant telle nouvelle,
> Desja sous le labeur à demy sommeillant,
> Qui au bruit de mon nom ne s'aille resveillant,
> Benissant vostre nom de louange immortelle. (7–8)[25]

We find the same sentiment in Spenser's *Sonnet LXXV*:

> my verse your vertues rare shall eternize,
> and in the hevens wryte your glorious name.[26]

Or in Shakespeare's *Sonnet XVIII*:

Nor shall Death brag thou wand'rest in his shade,
When in eternal lines to time thou grow'st;
So long as men can breathe or eyes can see,
So long lives this and this gives life to thee.[27]

This confidence in the lasting appeal of one's verse and this willingness to acknowledge authorship certainly find their noblest expression in Milton's *Paradise Lost*, and the latter attitude has lasted to this day with unabated vigour.

In contrast to their followers, mediaeval writers often seemed most eager to minimize their own contribution and belittle the quality of their work. Chrestien de Troyes, for example, assures us that he found the story for his *Cliges* already written in another book:

Ceste estoire trovons escrite,
Que conter vos vuel et retreire,
An un des livres de l'aumeire
Mon seignor saint Pere a Biauvez.[28]

The author of the *Nibelungenlied* likewise writes that he is merely retelling a tale recorded 'in alten mæren',[29] and Wolfram von Eschenbach insists several times in his *Parzival* that he does nothing more creative than translate the words of 'Kyôt der meister wol bekant'.[30] The expression 'co dist la geste' used as a means of denying creative authorship is among the most common tags in the Old French epic, and Chaucer's assertion that his *Troilus and Criseyde* simply retells a story by Lollius remains one of the most belaboured puzzles with students of English literature.

Like his predecessors, Lydgate disclaims his authorship time and time again. He presents *The Churl and the Bird*[31] as a straight translation:

And heere I cast unto my purpoos
Out of Frenssh a tale to translate
Which in a pamphlet I rade and sauh but late. (33–35)

If we accept his own word, his only concern in composing the *Troy Book* is to translate Guido's Latin 'as nyghe as ever [he] may' (prologue, 375), so as to comply with a request from the future Henry V:

> the worthy prynce of Walys
>
> . . . . .
>
> . . . me commaunded the drery pitus fate
> Of hem of Troye in englysche to translate,
> The sege also and the destrucccioun,
> Lyche as the Latyn maketh mencioun,
> For to compyle, and after Guydo make,
> So as I coude, and write it for his sake,
> Bycause he wolde that so hyghe and lowe
> The noble story openly wer knowe
> In oure tonge, aboute in every age,
> And ywriten as wel in oure langage
> As in Latyn and in Frensche it is. (Prologue, 1002–15)

His *Siege of Thebes* attempts only to do justice to his 'auctour' (199), *Guy of Warwick* is written precisely 'As the cronycle breefly doth compile' (281), and the *Fabula Duorum Mercatorum*[32] relates everything 'as the stoory tellith' (894). It is interesting that, although he opens his *Fall of Princes* with a defence of innovation and a justification of Laurent de Premierfait's additions to and departures from Boccaccio's text, Lydgate insists that his own translation will be scrupulously faithful to its original:

> Yit fro the trouthe shal I nat remue,
>
> But on the substance bi good leiser abide,
> Afftir myn auctour lik as I may atteyne,
> And for my part sette eloquence aside. (I, 231–4)

Lydgate is likewise a vigorous user of the topos of affected modesty. The instances of self-depreciation in his poetry are much stronger and elaborate than, say, John Barbour's purely conventional worry whether his 'wyt mycht suffice' to compose the *Bruce*[33] or Gower's assertion that his 'wittes ben to smale' for the task of writing the *Confessio Amantis* (Prologue, 81). For example, at the beginning of his *Isopes Fabules*,[34] which is believed to have been completed before 1400, he begs us accept his provincial origin as an excuse for his lack of rhetorical dexterity:

And, though I have no rethorik swete,
Have me excusyd: I was born in Lydgate;
Of Tullius gardeyn I passyd nat the gate,
And cause why: I had no lycence
There to gadyr floures of elloquence. (31–5)

The envoy to *The Churl and the Bird*, composed perhaps a little earlier,[35] is especially typical of his manner:

Go, litel quaier, and recomaunde me
Unto my maistir with humble affeccioun;
Beseche hym lowly, of mercy and pite,
Of thi rude makyng to have compassioun;
And as touchyng thi translacioun
Out of the Frenssh, howevyr the Englysh be,
All thyng is seide undir correccioun. (379–85)

Isopes Fabules and *The Churl and the Bird* are early works, written during Lydgate's most mediaeval period. More than fifty years later, however, we still find him practising affected modesty when he begins his *Secrees of Old Philisoffres* with an apology for the 'rudnesse of [its] style'.[36] I have mentioned earlier the epithet 'dull' which he applies to himself in the *Troy Book*. The conclusion to the prologue of that work tells us something more about the spirit in which he offers the product of his labour to the reader:

Al-be that I ne can the weye goon
To swe the floures of [Guido's] eloquence,
Nor of peyntyng I have noon excellence
With sondry hewes noble, fresche, and gay—
So riche colours biggen I ne may—
I mote procede with sable and with blacke.
And in enewying wher ye fynde a lak,
I axe mercy or I fro yow twynne. (II, 192–9)

Lydgate expresses similar sentiments in the *Fall of Princes*. At times the protestations of rhetorical inadequacy with which he generously equips his poem sound like mere formalities:

Though that I have lak off eloquence,
I shall procede in this translacioun,
Fro me avoiding al presumpcioun,
Lowli submyttyng every hour and space
Mi reud language to my lordis grace. (I, 437–41)

At other times, however, his tone and his images are convincing enough to convey sincerity:

> Lik a pilgrym which that goth on foote,
> And hath non hors to releve his travaile,
> Hot, drie, and wery, and fynde no boote
> Off welle cold, whan thrust hym doth assaile,
> Wyn no licour, that may to hym availe,
> Riht so fare I, which in my besynesse
> No socour fynde my rudnesse to redresse. (III, 1–7)

This earnest belittling of his own talent brings out an important difference in attitude between Lydgate and Chaucer. Like his follower, the older poet makes ample use of the topos of affected modesty; but, unlike him, he obviously does so with his tongue in his cheek, as in the invocation to Apollo with which he opens the third book of the *House of Fame*:

> O God of science and of lyght,
> Appollo, thurgh thy grete myght,
> This lytel laste bok thou gye!
> Nat that I wilne, for maistrye,
> Here art poetical be shewed;
> But for the rym ys lyght and lewed,
> Yit make hyt sumwhat agreable,
> Though som vers fayle in a sillable;
> And that I do no negligence
> To shewe craft, but o sentence.
> And yif, devyne vertu, thow
> Wilt helpe me to shewe now
> That in myn hed ymarked ys—
> Loo, that is for to menen this,
> The Hous of Fame for to descryve—
> Thou shalt se me go as blyve
> Unto the nexte laure y see,
> And kysse yt, for hyt is thy tree.
> Now entre in my brest anoon! (1091–1109)

The comic tone of the invocation results from the disparity between the immense magnitude of the power invoked and the insignificance of the task required. The god 'of science and of lyght' is asked to exercise nothing less than his 'grete myght' in order to help along a 'lytel . . . bok', whose principal deficiency is the occasional lack of a syllable; and the poet will be so grateful for this trifling contribution that he will think nothing of exposing himself to public laughter by rushing out to kiss the first laurel tree he encounters. If the god has any sense of humour, we have no doubt that he will do as requested right then and there. In effect, all this wonderfully ridiculous invocation tells us is that the poet is in no way ashamed of his product, even though this or that line may 'fayle in a sillable'.

In contrast to Chaucer, Lydgate often leaves us with the impression that he honestly deplores the lameness of his verse, as in the following passage from *Troy Book*:

> And trouthe of metre I sette also asyde;
> For of that art I hadde as tho no guyde
> Me to reduce, when I went awronge:
> I tok none hede nouther of shorte nor longe. (II, 181–4)

One finds it hard not to agree with Joseph Schick that the foregoing lines, 'if they do not reflect great credit upon [Lydgate's] metrical art, are at least delightfully candid'.[37]

The radical difference between the two attitudes expressed above gives us an idea of the extent of the disappointment felt by Percy, Ritson, and their followers if they searched the works of Lydgate in hope of finding Chaucer. They would probably have felt an equal disappointment if they had come to Chaucer with the expectation of finding Milton: they would surely have thought the invocation to Apollo a dismal failure to reach the appropriate high seriousness of tone, and their verdict might have proved even harsher than that of Matthew Arnold.

Contrary to the common belief that Lydgate's references to Chaucer point to an entire life misspent in vain attempts to imitate the master, these references are simply means of giving an immediate and personal quality to the conventional topos of affected modesty. The early fifteenth century recognized Chaucer as the first great English poet, and it is not altogether inconceivable that the young Lydgate had known him in person.[38] At any rate, we have seen above that he remained in lasting and close contact with his family. It seems therefore quite normal that he should have studied Chaucer assiduously enough to consider him his master even if he had never intended to imitate him at all. There is a vast difference between, on the one hand, attempting to imitate an author and, on the other hand, acknowledging his superiority, studying his works, and citing and quoting them.

Since the systematic use of footnotes and quotation marks did not become widespread until very recently, the modern reader does not always find it easy to tell whether an early author is imitating a predecessor or merely quoting him. Lydgate, however, makes his intention quite plain as he refers to Chaucer in the *Troy Book*:

> [I] seke his boke that is left behynde,
> Som goodly worde therin for to fynde
> To set amonge the crokid lynys rude
> Whiche I do write. As, by similitude,
> The ruby stant so royal of renoun
> Withinne a ryng of copur or latoun,
> So stant the makyng of hym, douteles,
> Among oure bokis of Englische pereles:
> Thei arn ethe knowe, thei ben so exellent;
> Ther is no makyng to his equipoent. (II, 4705–14)

Even in a passage of the *Lyf of Our Lady* where he bitterly deplores that Chaucer's death had deprived him of sorely needed guidance, he gives us no ground for assuming his intention to emulate the master:

> [Chaucer] fonde the floures firste of retoryke
> Our rude speche only to enlumyne,
> That in our tunge was nevere noon hym like;
> For as the sonne dothe in hevyn shyne
> In mydday spere doune to us by lyne,
> In whose presence no ster may apere,
> Right so his dytes withoutyn any pere
>
> Every makyng withe his light disteyne
> In sothefastenesse, whoso take the hede.
> Wherefore no wondre though my hert pleyne
> Upon his dethe, and for sorowe blede
> For want of hym nowe in my grete nede
> That shulde alas conveye and directe
> And with his supporte amende eke and corecte

The wronge traces of my rude penne
There as I erre and goo not lyne right.
But for that he ne may not me kenne,
I can no more but with all my myght,
With all myne hert and myne inwarde sight,
Pray for hym that liethe nowe in his cheste
To God above to yeve his saule goode reste. (II, 1635–55)[39]

In consonance with the topos of affected modesty, many of Lydgate's references to Chaucer are explicitly intended to clear their author from the charge of emulation and to emphasize his inability to follow in his predecessor's tracks. Turning once again to the *Troy Book*, for instance, we find an evaluation of the respective worth of each poet as Lydgate sees it:

For in makyng [Chaucer] dranke of the welle
Under Pernasso, that the Musis kepe;
On whiche hylle I myghte never slepe
Unnethe slombre, for whiche, alas, I pleyne. (III, 554–7)

And we read in the same poem his categorical opinion concerning the futility of imitation:

Whan we wolde [Chaucer's] stile counterfet,
We may all day oure colour grynde and bete,
Tempre our azour and vermyloun;
But al I holde but presumpcioun—
It folweth nat, therfore I lette be. (II, 4715–19)

In the *Fall of Princes*, he likewise pleads innocent of any presumption to tread on Chaucerian grounds:

Thyng onys said be labour of Chauceer
Wer presumpcioun me to make ageyn. (VI, 3627–8)

And when, in the same poem, he declines to elaborate upon the story of Philomela and her sister, it is for precisely the same reason:

Ther pitous fate in open to expresse,
It were to me but a presumpcioun
Sithe that Chaucer dede his besynesse
In his Legende, as maad is mencioun,
Ther martirdam and ther passioun
For to reherce. (I, 1793–8)

Just as Lydgate exploits the topos of affected modesty from one end of his literary career to the other, so he shows a lasting fondness for the device of mediaeval narrators which rhetoricians have termed *pauca e multis*. In practice, this simply consists in assuring the reader that the preceding or following narration, as the case may be, is a mere sampling of the subject matter, whose immense bulk defies inclusion in the present work.[40] More often than not, the presence of this device may be considered an indication that the writer has exhausted his fund of knowledge and prefers not to say so. About 1412 we find Lydgate using it in the *Troy Book* when, after listing the labours of Hercules, he dismisses the matter with the statement, 'Of this mater more what schulde I seyn' (I, 617). Some eight years and several thousand lines later he declines to add anything to Guido's text for fear that it be 'Lik a maner of presumpcioun' (V, 3365). Again in the *Fall of Princes*, he gives us only the barest gist of the story of Thebes and sends us to his own *Siege of Thebes* for the details:

> Al to declare, me semeth it is no neede,
> For in the Siege of Thebes ye may it reede. (I, 3723–4)

Lydgate occasionally makes joint use of the *pauca e multis* device and the modesty theme, as, for instance, when he explains that the inadequacy of his own rhetoric prevents him from including in the *Troy Book* a full description of King Cethes' feast:

> I wante connynge, by ordre to discrive
> Of every cours the diversytes,
> The straunge sewes, and the sotiltes
> That wer that day servid in that place.
> Hath me excused, though I lightly passe,
> Though I can not al in ordre seyn;
> Myn Englische is to rude and eke to pleyn
> For to enditen of so highe a thing. (I, 1556–63)

Thus Lydgate's narrative technique may be said to preserve to the end some of the outstanding features of the mediaeval tradition. To this observation, we may add another related one: although the language of his poetry moves decidedly toward Modern English,[41] his versification remains predominantly mediaeval. Scholars have demonstrated not only that his metrics are basically Chaucerian,[42] but that his favourite line can be traced as far back as the *Poema Morale*.[43]

The materials considered in this chapter warrant one generalization: Lydgate's early works were typically mediaeval both in content and in execution, and his rhetoric remained at least partly mediaeval to the very end of his career. We shall have occasion to return to this topic. Meanwhile we may reasonably assume that this adherence to the practices of mediaeval rhetoric has done very little to discourage literary critics from trying to evaluate Lydgate according to the standards normally applied to Chaucer and the Middle Ages.

Chapter Five

CLASSICAL ANTIQUITY

AS LYDGATE ADVANCED in age his attitude toward classical antiquity changed from that which we usually attribute to the Middle Ages to that which we consider indicative of the Renaissance. His early secular works pose no problem in this respect, for they simply reveal a total lack of concern for the classical past. A pious reference to Aesop in the prologue to *Isopes Fabules* only shows that Lydgate knows little about the Phrygian post, whom he seems to confuse with his Latin translator, Phaedrus:

> Unto purpos the poete laureate
> Callyd Isopus dyd hym occupy
> Whylom in Rome to plese the senate,
> Fonde out fables, that men myght hem apply
> To sondry matyrs, yche man for hys party,
> Aftyr theyr lust, to conclude in substaunce,
> Dyverse moralytees set out to theyr plesaunce. (8–14)

The first literary expression of his awareness of classical mythology is the description of a woodland spring in the *Complaint of the Black Knight*:

> The water was so holsom and so vertuous
> Throgh myghte of erbes grouynge ther beside;
> Nat lyche the welle wher as Narcissus

Islayn was thoro vengeaunce of Cupide,
Wher so covertely he dide hide
The greyn of deth upon eche brynk,
That deth mot folowe, who that evere drynk;

Ne lyche the pitte of the Pegace,
Under Parnaso, wher poetys slept;
Nor lyke the welle of pure chastite,
Whiche as Dyane with her nymphes kept,
When she naked into the water lept,
That slowe Acteon with his houndes felle,
Oonly for he cam so nygh the welle. (85–98)

These references, however, are of no serious consequence for our purpose. Since they are frankly meant to put the reader in mind of unfortunate love stories and act as a preface to a complaint of love, we may assume them to be part of the paraphernalia of courtly love which Lydgate inherited from his immediate predecessors; and the same argument applies to references, later in the poem, to other men and women of antiquity who suffered for love. In the *Book of the Duchess*, Chaucer had prefaced the main episode with the story of Ceyx and Alcyone. Much earlier Thomas de Hales, who was certainly untouched by classical influence, had already used similar references in his *Love Run* to illustrate the transience of earthly love and encourage his audience to turn to God.

One incidental remark may be permitted here concerning the use to which Lydgate puts his reference to the fates of Narcissus and Actaeon. By insisting that the well beside which he stands is *not* that which caused the unhappy ends of these men, he strongly suggests that the Black Knight's fate will not be the same as theirs, and thus firmly establishes the tone of his poem as that of a love complaint rather than that of the tragedy into which it might otherwise turn.

The *Troy Book* is the first unquestionably authenticated major work in which Lydgate must commit himself on classical antiquity. Since it is a translation, we have to determine to what extent it expresses the poet's own opinions and attitudes and to what extent it merely repeats those in Guido delle Colonne's *Historia*.

Whereas accurate translation seems to have been with us since times immemorial, objective translation is a relatively new phenomenon. Hartmann von Aue's *Iwein*, composed about 1200, is a case in point. Hartmann sets out to translate Chrestien de Troyes' *Yvain* into German, and comparison of the two texts often reveals the meticulous exactitude with which he has conducted his project. Yet the two poems are vastly different. The skilful additions which the German poet makes at strategic points so radically transform the lesson of the delightful romance of love and adventure that the story now revolves around the highly moral concepts of moderation (*mâze*) and faithfulness (*triuwe*). For instance, the hero's inordinate passion for jousting is so clearly developed into the grave crime of excess (*unmâze*) that its culimination into Iwein's failure to return home at the appointed date now appears as the perpetration of the heinous crime of unfaithfulness (*untriuwe*), and the subsequent loss of his wife's affection becomes the just and awful retribution which drives him into madness and temporary exile from the society of men. The spirit of the episode reminds us rather of the uncontrollable passion (*desmesure*) which drives the hero of *Raoul de Cambrai* to his tragic doom than of the charmingly subtle motivation of Chrestien's characters. We may, therefore, say of Hartmann that his translation is accurate and yet utterly subjective, so that whatever opinions we read in his work must be his own rather than Chrestien's.[1]

Chaucer illustrates another kind of accurate yet subjective rendering of a foreign text. When, in the *House of Fame*, he translates the opening lines of Virgil's *Aeneid* his English is faithful to the Latin in meaning, if not in tone:

> I wol now singen, yif I kan,
> The armes, and also the man
> That first cam, thurgh his destinee,
> Fugityf of Troy contree,
> In Itayle, with ful moche pyne
> Unto the strondes of Lavyne. (143–8)

One hundred and fifty-two lines later, however, he has Dido utter a complaint on male trickery the like of which surely never occurred to Virgil. He explicitly acknowledges Dido's utterance as his own creation; yet his interpretation so colours the narrative that the idea the reader gets of the *Aeneid* is that of a mediaeval love romance.

Lydgate follows the practices of both Hartmann and Chaucer: he generally stays with his original, but makes whatever alterations seem feasible to ensure that the final product does not clash with his own views; when the changes he wishes to make clearly betray the original text he often intrudes explicitly upon his author to give his own version of the events described or to explain what he considers their true significance. Of course, my account is intended as a generalization to which one will find many exceptions. In dealing with a poet who included among his translations such monumental and dissimilar pieces as Guido delle Colonne's *Historia Destructionis Troiae*, Guillaume de Deguileville's *Pelerinage de la Vie Humaine*, and Laurent de Premierfait's French adaptation of Boccaccio's *De Casibus*, the *Des Cas des Nobles Hommes et Femmes*, we should certainly not expect to find unswerving adherence to one rigid method of translation.

Lydgate shifts methods even within individual pieces. For instance, when Laurent translates from Boccaccio the story of Jason and Medea, he begins with a digression on the ever-increasing size of human population and its concomitant increase in misfortunes:

> Ainsi comme par diverses successions et generations d'hommes et femmes l'humain lignage qui se espandit ca et la avoit presque occupe toute espace de terre, aussi fortune a monstre qu'elle estoit dame des choses perissables et mondaines par les divers tournoyements et par la misere et povrete dont elle a travaile et batu plusieurs hommes et femmes: car ainsi comme je par necessite avoye laissse trespasser plusieurs aages sans rien escripre entre ung malheureux et l'autre pource que jay troube peu de cas malheureux advenus qui fussent tesmoignez en escript. Aussi pource que les hommes sont maintenant multipliez et accruez, je me voy environne d'une grant compaignie de nobles hommes et femmes plorans pour leur cas malheureux. Et quant je queroye ung malheureux pour racompter son cas, plusieurs vindrent devant moy.[2]

Lydgate in the *Fall of Princes* translates this passage most freely and follows the dictum of his better taste in reducing it to nine verses:

> When John Bochas was most diligent
> To considre the successiouns
> Off lynages, with all his hool entent,
> In his writyng and descripciouns
> To compile the generaciouns
> Of many noble, famous of estat—
> I meene off such as were infortunat—
>
> In his serchyng he fond not a fewe
> That were unhappi founde in ther lyvyng. (I, 2171–9)

Not only does the English omit much awkward material, but it shifts the point of view from the first person to the third and informs the reader of the speaker's identity, thus giving credit where it is due.

With the next line, however, Lydgate turns to a much closer kind of translation. The French reads, 'et devant les autres estoit Oetha, roy de l'isle de Colcos, que les gens cuyderent estre le filz du Soleil pour la noblesse et grandeur de luy ou pour la pesplendisseur de ses richesses qui encore ne avoient este veues aucune part si grans comme ledit Oetha les avoit. Cestuy Oetha souvent de son noble et riche estat mauldissoit en soy complaignant la venue de Jason' (p. 147). The English conveys practically the same information:

> To his presence anoon ther gan hem shewe
> A multitude ful pitousli weepyng,
> Amongis which, ful doolfulli pleynyng,
> Cam first Oetes, and hath his compleynt gunne,
> King of Colkos and sone onto the sunne.
>
> For off Phebus, which is so briht and cleer,
> Poetis write that he was sone and heir,
> Because he was so myhti off power,
> So fressh, so lusti, so manli, and so feir;
> But off Fortune he fill in gret dispeir,
> Cursyng his fate and his destyne,
> When Jason first entrid his cuntre. (I, 2180–91)

Making the necessary allowances for the shift of person already mentioned, for the changes which we may expect from the translation of prose into verse, and for the contrast between Lydgate's carefully worded sentences and Laurent's stylistic carelessness, we detect only one difference between the two documents, and it is rather insignificant. Whereas the French says of Oetes that people *thought* he was son of the sun, the English tells us that he *was* 'sone unto the sunne'. We shall see later that Lydgate is not always above flatly contradicting the author whom he translates and not giving the least indication thereof.

These observations do much more credit to Lydgate's determination to express his own views than they do to his accuracy as a translator, and they add evidence to Willard Farnham's statement that his translations reveal 'manly independence'.[3] For our immediate purpose, they give us the assurance that the opinions expressed in his translations are those which he endorses. Otherwise they simply would not be there.

The prevalent attitude toward classical antiquity which we find in the *Troy Book* is identical to that which we found earlier in the *Gest Hystoriale of the Destruction of Troy*, which, we recall, was also translated from Guido's *Historia*. Like most mediaeval historians, Guido had often painted the pagan poets in a thoroughly unflattering light, and Lydgate enthusiastically reproduces the picture, especially where Homer is concerned:

> These Poets han contreved by false transumpsioun
> To hyde trouthe falsely under cloude,
> And the sothe of malys for to schroude,
> As Omer dide, the whiche in his writyng
> Ifeyned hathe ful many divers thyng
> That never was, as Guydo lyst devise. (Prologue, 264–9)

The liberties which he allows himself in the translation are often aimed at darkening the already shady character allotted the ancient poets in the *Historia*. At one point, for example, Guido reproaches Homer with having allowed the gods to take sides and participate physically in the Trojan War: 'Inter quos suis diebus maxime auctoritatis Homerus apud grecos ejus hystorie puram et simplicem veritatem in versuta vestigia variavit fingens multa que non fuerunt aliter transformando.

Introduxit enim deos quos coluit antiqua gentilitas impugnasse trojanos et cum eis fuisse velut viventes homines debellatos cujus errorem postmodem poete curiosus insecuti ut darent intelligi non solum Homerum fuisse fictionum auctorem multa deludia scribere presumpterunt in libris eorum.'[4] Lydgate changes very little in this statement, but he succeeds in making Homer's fault appear even more hateful:

> And thingys done in another wyse
> He hathe transformed than the trouthe was,
> And feyned falsely that goddis in this caas
> The worthy Grekis holpen to werreye
> Ageyn Troyens, and howe that thei were seye
> Lyche lyfly men amonge hem day by day.
> And in his dites that were so fresche and gay,
> With sugre wordes under hony soote,
> His galle is hidde lowe by the rote,
> That it may nought outewarde ben espied. (prologue, 270–9)

When, after dutifully listing the pagan deities found in the *Historia*, he classifies all of them as 'the goddis of fals mawmetrie' (II, 5825) he clearly shares the view of classical antiquity expressed more than three hundred years earlier by the author of the *Chanson de Roland*.[5] The contrast between the attitude toward the gods in the *Troy Book* and that which we have already found in Gavin Douglas's *Eneados* is evident from Lydgate's admonition that good Christians should have only scorn for them:

> For by techyng of al holy chirche,
> The holy doctryne and tradiciouns,
> We shal dispise swiche oppiniouns,
> Whiche of the fende wer founde nat of late. (II, 5830–3)

He himself follows his own admonition when, much later in the poem, he abandons Guido's text to call the wrath of God upon the pagan deities:

> I praie to God yeve hem alle sorwe,
> Wherso thei ben, withinne or withoute!
> I noon except of the false route—
> Satorn nor Mars, Pallas nor Juno,
> Jupiter, Mercurius, nor Pluto,

Nouther Flora, that doth the floures sprede,
Nouther Bachus. (IV, 6948–54)

He carries on the diatribe for more than fifty lines, and in the process damns the entire Pantheon, not omitting a single satyr or dryad, 'Nor other goddes—nouther more ne lesse' (IV, 6990).

The instances discussed above are only a sampling of the attitude expressed throughout the poem, but they add evidence to the arguments of the many literary historians who have looked upon the *Troy Book* as a thoroughly mediaeval piece of work[6] and found in it the influence of Isidore of Seville, Peter Comestor,[7] Benoit de Sainte More,[8] Jacobus de Cessolis,[9] and other mediaeval authors.[10]

It is important to note, however, that a few scholars have occasionally detected in the poem the influence of classical authors[11] as well as isolated signs pointing toward Renaissance humanism.[12] The opening lines are noteworthy in this respect. Although the invocation to Mars may faintly echo the first stanza of Chaucer's *Anelida and Arcite*, and although the god will later be the object of Lydgate's indignation (IV, 4440 ff.), the tone of the passage is of the kind which we might expect to find at the beginning of a Renaissance epic:

O myghty Mars, that wyth thy sterne lyght
In armys hast the power and the myght,
And named art from est til occident
The myghty lorde, the god armypotent,
That, wyth schynyng of thy stremes rede,
By influence dost the brydel lede
Of chevalry, as sovereyn and patrown

. . . . .

So be myn helpe in this grete nede
To do socour my stile to directe. (prologue, 1–30)

The expression of unqualified respect for classical antiquity is a rare exception in the *Troy Book*; but it already suggests a faint glimmer of an attitude which was to stay with Lydgate and become the rule in his *Fall of Princes*.

In the *Troy Book* Lydgate introduces Ovid as a clever liar and only begrudgingly admits that Virgil may have occasionally spoken the truth:

Ovide also poetycally hath closyd
Falshed with trouthe, that maketh men ennosed
To whiche parte that thei schal hem holde—
His mysty speche so hard is to unfolde,
That it entriketh rederis that it se.
Vergile also, for love of Enee,
In Eneydos rehersyth moche thyng,
And was in party trewe of his writyng. (prologue, 299–306)

In the *Fall of Princes*, on the contrary, Ovid becomes a composer of poems with 'moral menyng' (IV, 96), and Virgil receives the kind of encomium which Lydgate thirty years before would have accorded no one except Chaucer:

Record I take of Virgile Mantuan,
That wrot the armys and prowesse of the man
Callid Eneas, whan he of hih corage
Cam to Itaill from Dido of Cartage.

Thre famous bokkis this auctour list compile,
Eneidoys first, which that dide excelle
In rethorik be sovereynte of stile.
He drank swich plente, this poete, as men tell,
Of the stremys that ran doun fro the well
Wrouhte bi tho sustres that be in noumbre nyne,
Prowesse of knihthod most cleerli to termyne.

For in that book he caste nat to faill,
With vois mellodious for to descryve ariht
The grete conquest of Rome and of Itaill
Wrouht bi Enee, the manli Troian kniht.
Whos vers notable yif so cleer a liht
Thoruh al the worlde, as in rethorik,
That among poetis was non unto hym lik.

He wrot also, this poete with his hond
Bi humble stile othir bookis tweyne,
Oon of pasture, the nexte of tilthe of lond,
The vers conveied with feet of metris pleyne.
Bi which thre labours a palme he dide atteyne.
To make his name throuh dites delitable
Above poetis to be most comendable. (IV, 67–91)

The pagan gods, whom we have just heard roundly damned as a 'false route', now become 'the hevenli goddis' (I, 5674). Apollo is no longer a despicable devil worshipped by Mohammedans, but rather 'the grete Appollo' (II, 3053), who renders judgment 'off equite and riht' (II, 3054). Lydgate still shows some suspicion about the means whereby the Delphic Oracle predicted the future (IV, 3608), but he has only admiration for the temple and expresses no scorn for those who worship there:

> Ther was a temple gret and merveilous,
> Bilt on a roche and on a hill off ston,
> Sacred tappollo callid Delphicus—
> In al Grece so gret a god was non.
> And offte sithe the peeple wolde gon
> Up to a theatre which that stood withoute,
> To have ansuere of that thei stood in doute. (IV, 3598–604)

When two henchmen of Cambyses attempting to rob the Temple of Jupiter Ammon are struck by lightning Lydgate highly approves of this punishment 'for ther presumpcioun' (III, 1663), and he later speaks with admiration of the time when 'Jupiter, for peeplis avauntages,/In silveren world conserved in clennesse' (VI, 1732–3). The predominant attitude expressed in the *Fall of Princes* toward the pagan gods is perhaps best suggested in the following account of the sacred laurel:

> To these goddis [Apollo and Jupiter], who can considre weel,
> Of old custum ther rihtis to meynteene,
> As for a thyng beyng perpetuel,
> Which fadeth nevere of nature, thus I meene,
> Isacrid is the fresshe laureer greene
> For causis tweyne grauntid to conquerours
> In marcial actis bi conquest maad victours.
>
> For the noblesse of this tre dyvyne
> Sheweth bi his odour in wisdam excellence;
> Bi the grennesse, which never doth declyne,
> Long abidyng of vertuous prudence;
> The rounde crowne betokneth providence,
> In signe onli, al knihtli governaunce
> Taketh his guerdoun of long contynaunce. (V, 533–46)

I have discussed earlier the connection between Lydgate and

Humphrey of Gloucester, whom *The Cambridge Medieval History* praises as one who 'must be regarded with gratitude as the restorer of classical learning in England'.[13] Near the beginning of the *Fall of Princes* Lydgate likewise lavishly praises his powerful patron as a nobleman of 'hih lettrure' who 'doth excelle/In understondyng alle othir off his age' (I, 385–6). Significantly, the evidence offered in support of this compliment is Humphrey's assiduity in the study of antiquity:

> His corage never doth appalle
> To studie in bookis off antiquite,
> Therin he hath so gret felicite
> Vertuously hymsilff to occupie. (I, 395–8)

Lydgate is as impressed with the Duke's sympathy for the ancients as he is with his having so thoroughly stamped out heresy that 'in this land no Lollard dar abide' (I, 403). When he praises not only his wisdom but also his 'manheed' (I, 400) he creates an embodiment of the ideal of *sapientia et fortitudo* which we have been used to associate with the Renaissance.[14] The passage discussed here must have been written about 1431.[15] Some nineteen years later we find Lydgate expressing for the last time his admiration for the ancients. When in the *Secrees of Old Philisoffres* he wishes to pay the highest possible compliment to Bishop Guy of Valence, he admiringly likens his style to that of Homer (378) and praises his familiarity with the Greek and Latin classics (428 ff.).

I have argued earlier that the Renaissance did not suddenly burst out to replace the Middle Ages in England, and that not all writers were equally affected by the new humanism. The same argument applies to individual poets, and Lydgate did not arbitrarily decide to accept classical antiquity the moment he brought his *Troy Book* to an end. Just as we have noted earlier that scholars have seen in that poem occasional signs of the coming Renaissance, so we must note that other scholars have convincingly argued the mediaeval quality of some of his later works;[16] but the most carefully documented observations may prove misleading if we take them at face value. In the *Fall of Princes*, for instance, we find that his approval of antiquity did not prevent Lydgate from writing (I, 6233–79; IV, 1107–

2002) what George Cary has called 'the most violent attack upon Alexander's whole personality to appear in Northern Europe. . . .'[17] But then, the English poem was intended for the perusal of that same Duke Humphrey whom we have already heard Lydgate congratulate on his vigour in cleansing England of heretics, so that we could not reasonably expect the poet to praise a pagan potentate whose 'surguedous pride' (IV, 1221) had been the object of repeated theological and moral condemnations.[18] In this respect one might add that his subsequent account of Alexander in the *Secrees of Old Philisoffres* is respectful in tone and presents a ruler wise enough to seek the advice of Aristotle because 'He wyst in soth that in philosophe . . ./He was expert' (487–9). Likewise, Robert Withington's somewhat sweeping but carefully supported observation that Lydgate's mummings were the first English dramatic works to make extensive use of classical allegory[19] is less helpful than it may seem, since the respective dates of the mummings have not yet been ascertained beyond question. For instance, we may recognize the pro-classical attitude of the *Fall of Princes* when Lydgate opens his *Mumming for the Mercers of London* with an address to 'Moost mighty Lord, Jubiter the Greet,/Whos mansyoun is over the sonnes beem' (1–2),[20] and goes on to devote the entire work to the process whereby the god sends his herald to London to greet the mayor of that city. We know that the mumming was composed several years after the *Troy Book*, but we cannot tell whether it was about the same time, or before, or after the *Mumming at Windsor*, which is usually considered a typically mediaeval piece and is concerned with the conversion of Clovis.[21]

Mere classical name dropping is not enough to earn a poet his place among the Renaissance humanists, and we have already seen that the Middle Ages made ample use of classical legends. A glance at the titles included in the so-called Matter of Rome the Great will likewise suggest the importance of classical history and pseudo-history in mediaeval literature, and it is common knowledge that the index of proper names in Chaucer lists an impressive number of classical entries. But Chaucer is not one to take the gods in earnest. More often that not his gods are merely part of a rhetorical machinery which may be tragic when in the *Troilus* he asks Tisiphone to assist 'the sorwful instrument/That helpeth loveres . . . to pleyne' (I, 10–11), or simply humorous when in the *Parliament of Fowls* he shows Venus 'well kevered . . ./Ryght with a subtyl coverchef of Valence' (271–2) among the other allegories of love; or they are part of his comic world, as when Morpheus refuses to awaken in the *Book of the Duchess* (178–85) or Criseyde states her conviction that 'goddes speken in amphibologies' (IV, 1406). In the vernacular literature of the Middle Ages the pagan gods are seldom respected for their theological and philosophical wisdom; instead they are likely to be domesticated as in *Sir Orfeo*, or moralized as in *Ovide Moralisé*. No one will claim that Lydgate's understanding of classical antiquity was superior to that which Curtius attributes to the Middle Ages in general,[22] but the frequency and earnestness of the allusions in his later works warrant the observation that he at least seems to have tried harder than his predecessors. The attitude reflected here becomes especially significant when we recall that his sources were predominantly typically mediaeval stuff. We shall see how in the *Siege of Thebes*, for instance, he methodically modified his original in favour of classical antiquity.

These observations do not effect a metamorphosis of Lydgate into an Oxford Humanist or a Guillaume Budé, but they allow us to say that the attitude detectable in his later works is of the kind that might have led the way to the humanists of the end of the century.

Chapter Six

THE PARAGON OF ANIMALS

WHEN E. M. W. TILLYARD examines the common notion that faith in the unmixed dignity of man is a distinctive characteristic of the Renaissance, he warns us that the case is not so clear-cut as we often assume. He reminds us that Hamlet calls man 'the paragon of animals', but also asks, 'What do such fellows as I do crawling between earth and heaven?' and concludes, 'we are arrant knaves, all.' Tillyard further points out that mediaeval theologians likewise believed in the dignity of man as a corollary to his having been created in the image of God.[1]

These are only reservations, and the remainder of Tillyard's argument takes for granted that the dignity of man was a more pervasive concern with the Renaissance than with any other period since classical antiquity. It is significant that the initial supporting evidence for his reservations is drawn from Shakespeare and mediaeval theology, thus suggesting, perhaps unwittingly, that the task of asserting man's dignity was the exclusive property of theologians until the advent of the Renaissance. In a way the suggestion is correct. The great writers of the English Renaissance assumed the intrinsic dignity of man despite his basic depravity. If we do away with this assumption, Spenser's *Faerie Queen* becomes at best a rather clever sequence of unrealistic chivalric adventures, and Milton's *Paradise Lost* deserves every word in George Bernard Shaw's satirical account of it as 'a long poem which neither I nor anyone else ever succeeded in wading through'.[2] By contrast, we would have to range far and wide to find a mediaeval secular epic devoted in large part to asserting the intrinsic value of man.

In another way, the suggestion is not so correct. The secular writers of the Middle Ages were passionately concerned with the dignity of man, but they were concerned with it only in so far as the dignity of an individual man could be expressed in relation to the ideals of Christian chivalry. The author of the *Chanson de Roland* is certainly concerned with the dignity of his hero. However, the reason for his concern is not that Roland is a man; it is, rather, that he is *a man who must suffer to come to terms with the ideals of Christian chivalry*. As he appears in the poem, he is interesting because he is almost hopelessly guilty of the mortal sin of pride. Otherwise he is a superb knight, so that only his lack of humility keeps him from achieving the dignity to which a creature in the image of God may aspire. We are allowed to follow step by step the increasingly tragic results of his removal from the ideal, and it is not until he has caused the massacre of his entire army rather than submit to the humiliation of calling for help that he realizes the extent of his fault. Then, in typically mediaeval fashion, he goes from the extreme of pride to the extreme of Christian humility as he begs mercy from the warriors who have fallen to uphold his reputation with the world. With humility comes human dignity and God's grace, so that the poet may now grant Roland the supreme reward of the dignity of man as he allows him an escort of angels to convey him to the eternal glory of heaven.

The author of the *Chanson* shows no such interest in the dignity of the twenty thousand men who die with Roland at Roncevaux. They have willingly sacrificed their lives in the performance of their duty, but they have never had to come to terms with the ideals of Christian chivalry. As such, whatever dignity they may claim is merely that which is intrinsic to every creature in the image of God, and the poet shows no more concern for it than Dante does for the souls of the sinless men who must spend eternity outside the gates of hell. The same thing may be said of Wolfram von Eschenbach's *Parzival*. Wolfram cares not a whit for whatever dignity may or may not belong to his hero through the mere fact that he happens to be a human being. However, he cares very much for the powerful emotions which turn Parzival into the antithesis of the ideals of Christian chivalry, and he is passionately concerned with the dignity to which he will accede the day when he finally humiliates himself to receive God's redemption. With or without the element of final redemption, the principle illustrated by the *Chanson de Roland* and *Parzival* is present in *Gormont et Isembart*, *Raoul de Cambrai*, *Girard de Rousillon* and countless other mediaeval epics.[3]

If we assume, as Tillyard believes the Renaissance did, that man possesses intrinsic dignity and that this dignity is worth our concern independently from the uses to which it is put, then we share in a mode of thinking quite alien to the Middle Ages as we usually imagine them. In a Christian society the assumption almost automatically leads to granting every human being the right to read the Bible and comment upon it, and we may conceivably reach the point where the greatest and most sophisticated poet of his own time and country feels a compulsion to justify the ways of God to *men*. In addition it becomes harder to evaluate people according to the category in which they belong, for such evaluation implies by definition a disregard for the intrinsic dignity of the individual human being. Accordingly, we can no longer prejudge a peasant as a peasant and a woman as a woman. We must now approach both with the same open mind which we used to reserve for Roland and Parzival. For example, we cannot very well prejudge Shakespeare's heroines according to their sex; each one must stand trial by herself according to the behaviour which the playwright has chosen for her part.

Because the Middle Ages supposedly held very firm views about the nature of the female sex as a whole, Lydgate's attitude toward women provides us with a particularly workable means of assessing his position in regard to the intrinsic dignity of man. My statement does not imply that all women in mediaeval literature fall in one category; we know that the heroine of the *Chastelaine de Vergy* is a lovely and unfortunate person, and her rival is a despicable creature in the tradition of Potiphar's wife. Nor are women in mediaeval literature bound to consistency of character within one poem; the heroine of the

Nibelungenlied is first introduced as such a lovable young girl that 'niemen was ir gram' (3, 2), but she eventually turns into the pitiless monster whom Dietrich von Bern can only describe as *vâlandinne*—she-devil (1748, 4). Nevertheless, the Middle Ages appear to have been bound by two mutually contradictory assumptions concerning womankind. One was the assumption of the monastery, according to which women were altogether abominable; the other was the assumption of the court, according to which women were unexceptionally wonderful. The two attitudes, it must be noted, were formalized and complementary. The expert on the subject, Francis Lee Utley, writes that 'formalized satire is coeval with formalized love' and that 'when the Middle Ages formalized love . . . the ambivalent hate was included in the formula'.[4]

At the root of the mediaeval monastery's attitude lay the remembrance that man had lost earthly paradise because of woman. Frederick W. Locke has summed up the case with clarity and succinctness: 'Behind this mediaeval attitude towards women was a monastic tradition whose influence upon letters and institutions cannot be overestimated. The angry denunciation against the perennial Eve is a cry that is heard throughout the period: every woman is *Eva rediviva*, the personification of the temptress through whom man originally fell from innocence.'[5] Andreas Capellanus is illustrative of this attitude when, after compiling a kind of field manual for courtly lovers, he devotes several pages to warning his audience against the perversity of women. Every woman, he argues, is a born liar, a miser, a slanderer, a glutton, a drunkard, a babbler, a breaker of promises, and a hopelessly arrogant creature. His list reads like a catalogue of all mortal and venial sins known to theologians, and he concludes it with the assertion that no woman is an exception to its strictures.[6] Such assumptions surely underlie Saint Bernard's warning, 'de feminis tuis suspectis quid agant ignoranciam queras. Postquam sciveris crimen male uxoris a nullo medico curaberis',[7] for which an early Scottish translator has given the following rendition:

This doctor sayis off wysdome in his saw,
Quhat sum ever mane happynis for to knaw
The wykytness and sorow of a wyfe,

Na medicine may mende hyme in his lyffe,
Na the dolowr of hyr that is his make
Be na science thar is na leche can slake.[8]

These and innumerable other such statements[9] bear out the Wife of Bath's famous observation that the mediaeval clergy has seldom been noted for enthusiastic approval of things feminine:

For trusteth wel, it is an impossible
That any clerk wol speke good of wyves,
But if it be of hooly seintes lyves. (*WBT*, 688–90)

In contrast to the monastery, the mediaeval nobility showed no reservations about women. On the contrary, the royal and baronial courts of England and western Europe seem to have devoted a considerable portion of their time to the theory and practice of courtly love. Since the central feature of courtly love was its insistence that the man must obey without delay or question the silliest whimsies of the woman,[10] the nobility could not logically be expected to have shared the monastery's views of womankind.

If we turn for a moment to thirteenth-century Germany, we find the kind of servility which courtly love required of a man clearly manifested in Ulrich von Lichtenstein's poetical autobiography, appropriately entitled *Frauendienst*.[11] At one point, we see Ulrich submitting to a painful surgical operation so that the shape of his mouth may conform to the wishes of his lady. As a result of this touching demonstration of obedience, he must go about with a bright green and extremely smelly ointment smeared over his lips and is forced to abstain from food so long that he nearly dies of starvation (I, 28, 2 ff.). Later in the poem he relates how he had a finger chopped off, mounted in gold, and delivered to the same woman in hope of winning her praise (I, 138, 25 ff.); and yet later he tells us that he thought nothing of disguising himself to look like the Goddess of Love and jousting his way from the shores of the Adriatic to the state of Bohemia for the same reason (I, 161, 3 ff.).

Ulrich took his women very seriously; and so did his English and French successors who, during the fourteenth century, worshipped Cupid at the courts of love and divided themselves into amorous factions holding as their emblem either the flower or the leaf of the daisy. In France we find Froissart and Deschamps dutifully turning out poems in honour of that flower. There, too, history affords us an embarrassing illustration of the prestige enjoyed by women at court: we see no less a literary figure than Guillaume de Machaut willingly make a poetic buffoon of himself for the sole amusement of the concupiscible Péronnelle d'Armentières, who seems to have given him just enough hope to keep him going until she tired of the game and turned to a younger man.[12]

Every reader of the *Legend of Good Women* remembers how, when Chaucer dared come forth with a few humorously uncomplimentary remarks about women and compounded the crime by showing no concern at all whether men 'ben with the leef or with the flour' (F, 72), the God of Love appeared in person to give him a severe reprimand:

> Thow art my mortal fo and me werryest,
> And of myne olde servauntes thow mysseyest,
> And hynderest hem with thy translacyoun,
> And lettest folk to han devocyoun
> To serven me. . . .
> Why noldest thow as wel han seyd goodnesse
> Of wemen, as thow hast seyd wikednesse? (G, 248–68)

The strong possibility that the God of Love was meant to represent actual critics of Chaucer[13] tells us something of the prestige which women enjoyed with the literary nobility of the fourteenth century.

It may well have been the practice of courtly love which placed noblewomen on such a pedestal that, at the turn of the fourteenth and fifteenth centuries, Christine de Pisan could earn a living by composing clever poems for the delight of the court of France. Even more telling is the fact that, when she wrote her *Dit de la Rose* to attack Jehan de Meung's antifeminist doctrines, Jehan de Montreuil and Gonthier Col—both secretaries to Charles VI—did not consider it beneath their dignity to enter into an epistolary controversy on the subject with her.[14]

Turning now to Lydgate, we become aware of a significant paradox: Lydgate was a monk and Lydgate was a court poet.

Consideration of the opinions about women which he expresses in his poetry suggests that he succeeded in keeping the two professions fairly distinct from each other; some of his poems are exclusively monastic in their attitude toward women, while others are exclusively courtly.

The monastic attitude is blatant in his *Examples Against Women*,[15] where he seriously looks upon women as the undeniable cause of human perdition:

> But whan Adam was ffallen in dotage
> And agayn God beganne to holden stryff
> Through excityng of Eve. . . . (17–19)

The spirit of his *Pain and Sorrow of Evil Marriage*,[16] adapted from the *De Conjuge non Ducenda*, is precisely that which we have seen illustrated in Saint Bernard's *De Cura Rei Famuliaris*:

> Glory unto God, laud and benysoun
> To John to Petir, and also to Laurence,
> Which have me take under proteccioun
> From the deluge of mortall pestilence
> And from the tempest of deedly violence,
> And me preserved I fell not in the rage
> Under the yoke and bondis of mariage. (1–7)

The rampant misogyny of the picture which follows in the same poem seems to come straight out of Andreas Capellanus's account:

> . . . Petyr, called the Corbelio,
> Affermyd pleynly how wyfes gladly be
> Dyvers of hert, full of duplicite,
> Right mastirfull, hasty and eke proude,
> Crabbed of language when thei lust cry lowde. (45–49)

Since Lydgate opens his poem with thanks to God and his saints who have spared him the fate that befell the husbands of the Wife of Bath, it is of interest that his final indictment shows women behaving in the very same manner as Chaucer's unforgettable character, who wore 'gaye scarlet gytes' (*WBT*, 559) to go on pilgrimage:

> They hem rejoise to see and to be sayne,
> And to seke sondry pilgremages,

At grete gaderynges to walken upon the playne
And at staracles to sitte on hie stages,
If they be ffaire, to shewe ther visages;
If they be ffowle of look or countenaunce,
They can amend it with plesaunt daliaunce.

Of ther nature they gretly hem delite
With holy fface fayned for the nones
In seyntnaries ther ffrendes to visite
More than for relikkes or any seyntis bones,
Though they be closed under precious stones,
To get hem pardoun, like there olde usages,
To kys no shrynes, but lusty yong images. (99–112)

At times Lydgate prefers sarcasm to straightforward condemnation. For instance his satirical *Beware of Doublenesse*[17] begins with a mock-commendation of feminine constancy:

This world is ful of variaunce
In every thing, whoo taketh hede,
That feyth and trust and al constaunce
Exiled ben, this is noo drede;
And safe oonly in womanhede,
I kan see no sykyrnesse. (1–6)

After thirty-two lines devoted to the instability of worldly things, he again insists, 'Save that woman be hool and pleyne' (39). Only when he assures us that 'Salamon was not so sage/To fynde in hem noo doublenesse' (63–64), do we at last perceive the real intention of the poem. Of course, the monastic audience of the Middle Ages would have grasped the satirical intent with the first mention of feminine steadfastness, for they knew that women were by definition the antithesis of that quality. The remainder of the poem requires no such knowledge of the female mind, for the sarcasm is as plain today as it was the day Lydgate wrote it down:

Sampson hadde experience
That women weren ful trewe founde
When Dalida of innocence
With shares gan his hede to rounde;
To speke also of Rosamounde,
And Cleopatris feythfulnesse,

The storyes pleynly wil confounde
Men that apeche her doublenesse. (81–88)[18]

As may be expected the attitude discussed here is well represented in the *Troy Book*, where Lydgate solemnly lectures on the fickleness of women:

For who was ever yit so mad or wood,
That ought of resoun conne aright his good,
To geve feith or hastily credence
To any woman, without experience,
In whom is nouther trust ne sikernesse.
Thei ben so double and ful of brotilnesse
That is is harde in hem to assure.

. . . . .

For if the trouthe inwardly be soughte
With the surpluse and remnaunte of her thoughte,
Men may ther the trewe patron fynde
Of inconstaunce, whos flaskisable kynde
Is to an fro mevyng as a wynde,
That Hercules were nat strong to bynde
Nouther Sampson, so as I bileve,
Wommanes herte to make it nat remeve.
For as the blase whirleth of a fire,
So to and fro thei fleen in her desire
Til thei accomplische fulli her delite. (I, 1845–75)

One need not be an expert in mediaeval literature to recognize here the sentiments expressed by the disgruntled Gawain near the end of *Sir Gawain and the Green Knight*:

Bot hit is no ferly thagh a fole madde
And thurgh wyles of wymmen be wonen to sorghe.
For so watz Adam in erde with one begyled,
And Salamon with fele sere, and Samson eftsones;
Dalyda dalt hym hys wyrde, and Davyth therafter
Watz blended with Barsabe, that much bale tholed. (2414–19)

Nor does the patently conventional quality of Lydgate's anti-feminism always result in triteness of execution. On the contrary, his *Ballade on an Ale Seller*[19] reveals that he can at times turn out a most effectively graphic description of the fatal charms used by women to lure innocent men to perdition:

Your callyng look, the sholdres ofte thwertyng,
Your brestis bare, I dar right weel assur,
Your lauhtir, and your sadde kissyng. . . . (8–10)

The monastic lesson is so vividly expressed here that the modern reader is reminded of Robert Browning's *Soliloquy of the Spanish Cloister*:

Simply glance at it, you grovel
Hand and foot in Belial's gripe. (59–60)

As is only natural for a monk, Lydgate seems to have had no qualms about expressing the monastery's attitude toward women. It is likewise natural that a court poet should express the attitude of the court on the same subject, and Lydgate seems to have performed this task with the same energy with which he performed the other. His avowedly profeminine works are without exception poems of courtly love, and the women therein receive all the conventional compliments which the audience of the time expected to hear. This woman has 'Fresshe lusty beaute, joyned with gentylnesse';[20] that other 'passethe of beaute Isaude and Eleyne';[21] yet a third accumulates 'bounte, beaute, shappe, and semelyhed/Prudence, wite, passyngly fairenesse'[22] and other similar qualities, including many of those specifically denied women by the monastery. When he needs specific instances to illustrate the feminine virtues, Lydgate does not hesitate to bless the very same women whom we have heard him damn in his misogynistic works. Thus, in *Of Her That Hath All Virtues*,[23] he seriously mentions 'Cleopatres abyding stabulnesse' (19), and admiringly refers to 'feyre Rosamounde' (22).

In one respect, however, Lydgate's courtly poetry reflects the influence of the monastery. We need no great insight to suspect that courtly love, with its lesson of adultery and its religion of love,[24] must have seemed extremely wicked business to the monastic mind. The problem has been investigated by Father Alexander J. Denomy, whose conclusion leaves no room for argument short of refutation: 'It is impossible to reconcile the tenets of Courtly Love with the Commandments of God, with Divine Will as interpreted by Saint Paul, with the teaching of Christ and of His Church.'[25] To be sure, precept and practice seldom agree with each other, and we know that the members of the clergy who lived at the courts of England and western Europe during the later Middle Ages did not commonly express violent abhorrence for the teachings of courtly love. But then, they were usually not compelled to write poems about it. Lydgate, on the other hand, had to satisfy the wishes of noble patrons who wanted precisely that kind of poetry, and we may assume that he did not remain unaware of the ambiguity of his situation.

Lydgate extricates himself from this ambiguous situation with the help of two simple devices: whenever his poetry dangerously verges on the religion of love, he inserts whatever unobtrusive statements might if necessary afford him a technical plea of not guilty; whenever his topic includes an erotic situation, he either stops short of the expected conclusion or he makes it ambiguous enough to leave the actual consummation of the sexual act to the reader's imagination.

Both devices are found in the *Complaint of the Black Knight*, where Lydgate makes an appeal to Venus:

> O feire lady! wel-willy founde at al,
> Comfort to carefull! O goddesse immortal!
> Be helpyng now and do thy diligence
> To let the stremes of thin influence
>
> Descende doune in furtheryng of the trouthe,
> Namely of hem that lye in sorow bounde;
> Shew now thy myght and on her wo have routhe
> Er fals Daunger sle hem and confounde. (627–34)

Taken out of context, this is an invocation to the pagan Goddess of Love and, accordingly, liable to the charge of heresy which Father Denomy justifiably brings against the practices of courtly love. Within context, however, the utterance simply reveals a clever play on words. A few lines before the poet has noticed a star shining in the west; it is 'Venus with her bemys clere' (614), named after the Goddess of Love. Since he has been deploring the Black Knight's unhappy fate in love, the sight gives him the idea of falling on his knees and addressing the star for the sake of the deity's jurisdiction over erotic matters:

> And even thus to her [i.e. the star] I gan to preie:
> 'O lady Venus! so feire upon to se.' (618–19)

Furthermore, he is careful to remind us a little later that his words are addressed, not to a real pagan deity, but indeed to a star: 'O glade sterre! O lady Venus myn' (639).

What Lydgate really expresses is the hope that the sentiment of love—perhaps even the desire for sexual experience—will drive the lady to grant her suitor's request before his passion kills him. Nor does he formulate a single explicit statement that might make his hope technically sinful in the monastic mind; for aught we know, he is merely hoping that the Black Knight will enter the state of holy matrimony with his beloved. If we assume—as Lydgate's audience probably did—that prospective matrimony has no special place in the poem and that the lover's wishes may be adulterous as well as not, we do so only because of our natural inclinations and our knowledge of the practices of courtly love.[26] Then it is we, and not the poet, who are disregarding the teachings of the Church. It is significant that the ultimate control of the situation rests explicitly, not in the hands of Venus, but in those of the Christian God. The lover may complain that Nature has made his lady too perfect for his own good, but he makes it clear that she has done so only because it was part of God's greater scheme:

> The myghty Goddesse also of Nature,
> That under God hath the governaunce
> Of worldly thinges commytted to her cure,
> Disposed hath thro her wyse purveaunce
> To yive my lady so moche suffisaunce
> Of al vertues, and therwithal purvyde
> To mordre Trouthe, hath taken Daunger to guyde. (491–7)

The extent of the caution exercised in the *Black Knight* is obvious if we compare it with a rather outspoken courtly poem by William IX of Aquitaine. In *Companho Faray un Vers Covinen* William asks for our advice on the dilemma that faces him. He has two fine mares for his saddle; they perform splendidly in all the required exercises, but they hate each other so fiercely that he cannot keep them both:

> Dos cavalhs ai a ma selha ben e gen;
> Bon son e adreg per armas e valen;
> Mas no'ls puesc amdos tener que l'us l'autre non cossen.[27]

We are not exactly surprised when we learn in the concluding line that the two horses that give their rider such pleasure are named respectively Agnes and Arsen.

We have noted earlier in this study that Lydgate's love poetry does not lack in erotic boldness. The erotic element, however, is never explicitly stated. Instead, we are supplied with all the images and allusions necessary to set our imagination working—as in the case of the *Floure of Curtesy*, where the sight of innumerable birds busily mating tells us precisely what the lover has in mind, though we read no explicit statement on the point—and the final interpretation is left to us. Had William IX followed a similar method, he would have left out the last line of his poem and allowed the reader to interpret on his own the perfectly obvious meaning of the equine image. Paradoxically, Lydgate's monastic deviousness often turns the eroticism of his poetry into a much more serious matter than it might otherwise be.

Whether openly or covertly, Lydgate expresses both the monastic and the courtly attitudes toward women; and in so far as he does so, he remains in the alleged tradition of the Middle Ages. However, he also expresses a third attitude which is that of the Renaissance as we have outlined it earlier in this chapter: women are human beings, and each human being must be judged according to his own merits.

Tillyard has remarked that even such a mediaeval work as the *Troy Book* occasionally reflects the attitude of the Renaissance toward women.[28] A glance at the work itself will justify that opinion, for we find Lydgate stating his conviction that there is no intrinsic difference in behaviour between the sexes. He recognizes that reliable observers have detected disturbing faults in women, but then, he adds, 'ofte tyme thei se men do the same' (I, 2110). We must be careful to differentiate the attitude implied in this statement from an apparently similar one in the *Roman de la Rose*, where Amis and the Vieille recount somewhat disturbing instances of male misbehaviour. Considering Amis's role in the poem, we cannot seriously expect him to side with the jealous husband, and the beating which the latter gives his wife by no means permits the conclusion that Jehan de Meung thinks men inherently as bad as women.[29] In fact, one is nearly tempted to draw the opposite conclusion from Amis's pious assertion that love and forced obedience never keep company—'. . . . onques amour e seignourie/Ne s'entrefirent compaignie' (8451–2)—for we recall that Chaucer puts the same statement in the mouth of the uncourtly Franklin who foolishly presumes to teach us a lesson in the art of courtly love: 'Love wol nat been constreyned by maistrye' (*FT*, 764). As for the Vieille, the ludicrous self-pity which she displays in relating her own life[30] clearly disqualifies her as a mouthpiece for the author's serious opinions. The stories which she tells of the unfaithfulness of Aeneas, Paris, and Jason must, I believe, be taken with a grain of salt. We must not forget that when the God of Love coerced Chaucer into retelling similar stories he unwittingly admitted that the *Roman de la Rose* would discourage all *wise* men from the love of women:

> Thou hast translated the Romaunce of the Rose,
> That is an heresye ayeins my lawe,
> And makest *wise folk* fro me withdrawe. (*LGW*, F, 329–31)

If 'wise folk' have withdrawn, then only fools are left to love women. Assuming the slip to be the God of Love's rather than Chaucer's, we know how the lesson of the *Roman de la Rose* was construed by its own translator; and we further guess that the stories which Chaucer tells as his 'penaunce' (F, 495) in the *Legend of Good Women* ought perhaps to be taken as the result of a courtly equivalent of theological attrition rather than actual contrition.

To return to the *Troy Book*, when Lydgate comments upon a particularly misogynistic passage in the text he is translating, his main objection is to Guido's practice of evaluating women as a category rather than as individual human beings:

> Thus techeth Guydo, God wot, and not I!
>
> . . . . .
>
> Whiche made nat, thorugh indiscrecioun,
> Of good nor badde noon excepcioun.
> He was to blame—foule mote he falle—
> For cause of oon to hindren alle. (III, 4343–60)

A few minutes later he refutes his author's generalization that all women are sexually promiscuous, and he again insists that what is true of them is likewise true of men:

For lak of oon alle are nought to blame,
And eke of men may be seide the same. (III, 4387–8)

In the final book of the poem he reminds the reader that, though some women have indeed proved despicable, many others have been admirable:

And though Guydo in his boke endite
The variaunce of Elayne or Cryseyde,
Or Medea, that for sorwe deyde,
Let ther agayn, of right and equite,
The wyfly trowthe of Penelope,
The maydenhed of yonge Policene,
And the goodness of Eccuba the quene,
Of Cassandra eke the stedfastnes—
And with al this, take the kyndenes
Of Pantasile, withoute variaunce,
And put al this togidre in balaunce,
And ye shal fynde, yif ye list accounte,
Maugre who grucchith, trouthe shal surmounte,
I dar aferme, and bere aweye the pris:
There wil no man replie that is wys;
He were to fable in his oppinioun. (V, 2204–19)

The same reluctance to generalize on the nature of any group of human beings is present in the *Fall of Princes*. Every woman in the poem is judged according to her own behaviour. Thus, Scylla is reproached with 'hir horrible deed' (I, 2601), Delilah is shown acting 'lich a serpent daryng under floures/Or lik a werm that wrotith on a tre' (I, 6433–44), and 'that cursid Jezebel' (II, 1723) is offered as a loathsome example of human wickedness. After relating how Phaedra's lies caused the death of Hippolytus, Lydgate allows himself a sweeping statement:

Wyves off talis been sumwhile inventiff
To suffre ther tunges falsli fleen at large. (I, 2838–9)

But he immediately retracts the generalization by excluding from it all good women:

I meene nothyng off wyves that been goode,
Nor off women that floure in innocence. (I, 2843–4)

Just as in the *Troy Book* Lydgate condemns Guido's generalizations on feminine viciousness, so in the *Fall of Princes* he disapproves of Boccaccio's generalizations on the same subject:

And treuli it doth me wit appall
Of this mateer to make rehersaile;
It is no resoun tatwiten women all,
Thouh on or too whilom dede faile;
It sittith nat, nor it may nat availe,
Hem to rebuke that parfit been and goode,
Ferr out off joynt thouh sum other stoode. (I, 6658–71)

Although he recognizes that some women have been wicked, he reminds the reader that many have led virtuous lives and ought not to lose their good repute for the sake of their less virtuous sisters:

Ful many on have cleene been al ther lyve,
Ondefouled kept ther virgynyte;
And summe coude ageyn alle vices stryve
Hem to conserve in parfit chastite,
Devoid off chaung and mutabilite.
Though sum other have therageyn trespacid,
The laude off hem is therewith nat diffacid. (I, 6679–85)

Again as in the *Troy Book*, he makes the point that men are not necessarily better than women:

And who that ever off malice list accuse
These celi women touchyng variaunce,
Lat hem remembre and in ther wittis muse
Men be nat ay stable in ther constaunce;
In this world heer is no perseveraunce,
Chaung is ay founde in men and women bothe. (I, 6686–91)

The individual judgments in these works are what we ordinarily expect from mediaeval monks. Any one of Lydgate's colleagues might conceivably commend 'of Hester the meeknesse' and reprove Delilah's 'fals apparence', as is done in the *Fall of Princes* (I, 6672; 6440); or approve of Constantine for ordering that Jesus be 'worsheped in every regioun' and disapprove of Julian the Apostate for becoming 'to Cristes lawe . . . mortal enmy' (*ibid.*, VIII, 1293; 1549). What distinguishes

Lydgate, however, is not the nature of these judgments, but the constant reiteration of his conviction that there is no intrinsic moral difference between the sexes. What further distinguishes him from his lay predecessors is the tone in which he expresses this conviction. With Chaucer, in particular, accounts of the wrongs of women and the misdeeds of men tend to leave the reader perplexed as to the poet's overall view of the subject; the pervading irony is such that, as E. Talbot Donaldson was the first to point out, 'Two points of view, in strict moral logic diametrically opposed, are somehow made harmonious in Chaucer's wonderfully comic attitude, that double vision that is his ironical essence.'[31] There is no such double vision in Lydgate, so that the tone is always in keeping with the stated purpose of the verse. When he writes on women from the monastic point of view the tone is frankly hostile; when he writes from the courtly point of view it is frankly laudatory; when he wishes to be satirical it turns into obvious sarcasm. Likewise, when he wishes to pass serious moral judgment in a work intended for that purpose the tone of his verse is one of complete earnestness. Because Lydgate is devoid of this 'habitually ironic expression, which is continually telling us either more or less than the actual words are saying' which Bertrand H. Bronson proposes as a key to Chaucer,[32] the reader has to accept his statements at their face value.

One cannot disregard Utley's argument that Lydgate's defences of women simply 'testify to a mixed audience'.[33] The explanation is convincing to a point, since the poet enjoyed the patronage of several noblewomen whom he may have wished to flatter;[34] yet it remains unsatisfactory on two counts. In the first place, by the time he wrote the *Fall of Princes* he was beyond doubt the chief literary figure of England. His fame had risen to such height that it has been said that the only reason why he did not become Poet Laureate is that the office did not yet exist. It seems improbable that a man in his position would have had to curry favour with anyone except the powerful Humphrey of Gloucester, under whose patronage the poem was composed. In the second place, these defences of women are not apologies for womankind as such; they are rather expressions of the humanistic belief that every human being has the right to be judged according to his own merits rather than according to preconceived ideas about a category to which he belongs through no fault of his own.

The observation that Lydgate is defending the individual rather than the category is the basis of the present argument. In this respect the monastic and courtly poems in which he either praises or damns the whole of womankind are of secondary importance, for the debate over the worth of women extended from the Middle Ages well into the Renaissance. The fact that 250 of the 400 antifeminist pieces tabulated by Utley are dated between 1500 and 1568 is revealing,[35] even if its significance is tempered by the awareness that the invention of printing has made it easier to preserve the documents of the Renaissance than those of the Middle Ages. With the exception of Thomas Elyot's *Defence of Good Women* on one side and John Knox's *First Blast of the Trumpet against the Monstrous Regiment of Women* on the other, however, the debate failed to attract the great vernacular writers of the latter period;[36] and, though the majority of humanists who wrote in Latin showed little zeal to enter the fray in behalf of women, Vives's *De Institutione Christianae Feminae* and Erasmus's *De Matrimonio Christiano* show that those whose influence is still acknowledged today took a sympathetic interest in the education of women.[37] Thus Renaissance humanism did little to alter the debate within its own context, but outside that context it did much to assert the intrinsic dignity of the individual human being. Utley, to turn to him once again, has neatly summed up the phenomenon:

> But as real people became heroes and heroines, as tragedy was transformed from a fall from a high place to a testimony to the dignity of the human spirit with all its flaws and all its blind spots, the old rigid notions of good and evil were of necessity altered, and *it was no longer possible for men of great or even of little genius to separate women and men into goatland and sheepfold*. . . . Throughout the Renaissance the old catalogues of good and evil women continue, but there seems to be a growing embarrassment in their use—realization, in short, that an argument which may be used so glibly on both sides of the question may also be of little worth to either.[38]

This embarrassment at the practice of separating women and

men into goatland and sheepfold represents precisely Lydgate's attitude in the *Fall of Princes*, where, if we accept Farnham's view on the subject, our poet was the first of his nation to give 'some recognition to famous women as tragic characters'.[39] In the *Troy Book* he had already expressed similar opinions for the benefit of Henry V; it is to be expected that he would repeat the experiment with renewed vigour in a work composed for Duke Humphrey, who was the most ardent patron of the humanists at the time. Had Lydgate really wished to cater to a feminine audience rather than express the views of the new humanism, he would surely have begun by eliminating from his poem the innumerable examples of feminine treachery which it contains.

Many years earlier, in the *Tale of the Wolfe and the Lamb*,[40] Lydgate had expressed the monastic conviction that God rewards men after death according to their individual deserts rather than according to the category in which they belong:

> As men deserve, they receve theyr guerdon:
> Onrepentaunte, the tyraunt goth to hell;
> The pore man with small possession
>
> . . . . .
>
> When he goth hens, hath heven to hys mede. (344–50)

In the *Fall of Princes* he now assures us that human beings need not wait for the bliss of heaven or the pains of hell to see their actions properly evaluated. Each one of them must be treated as a separate entity, for regardless of sex or station in life 'Summe be vicious, summe in vertu shyne' (IX, 3273), and they must be judged accordingly:

> For which lat men deeme as thei mut needis,
> Nat afftir berthe but afftir the deedis. (VI, 601–2)

In the *Wife of Bath's Tale*, we recall, Chaucer had already affirmed that 'he is gentil that dooth gentil dedis' (1170);[41] but the utterance is loaded with the sort of irony which Donaldson and Bronson find in its author, for it is placed in the mouth of a woman 'so loothly, and so cold also,/And therto comen of so lough a kynde' (1100–1) grotesquely attempting to use logic in order to convince a young, handsome, and noble knight to make love to her and like it.

This belief that every human being has a right to be regarded as a separate entity is so strong with Lydgate that on at least one occasion we may detect its influence in such an unlikely place as a poem of courtly love. With the exception of pieces devoted to the sorrows of Dido and the other good women who suffered the consequences of masculine fickleness, the poetry of courtly love normally concentrates upon the sundry trials which male lovers are likely to undergo in their quest for amorous experience. The convention which places the woman on a quasi-unattainable pedestal tends to blind poets to the fact that she, too, may be an individual human being with emotions of her own, and that she may suffer through the very convention of which she is supposedly the beneficiary. I do not mean that the poetry of courtly love never depicts the suffering of women. No one will deny that Chaucer's Criseyde suffers when she attempts to justify her betrayal of Troilus with the self-reassuring statement that she means well; Isolde certainly suffers when she collapses upon her dead lover; and so does Engeltrut, in Konrad von Wurzburg's *Engelhard*, when the despicable Ritschiert von Engellant exposes her love affair with Engelhard. However, their sufferings are not caused by the clash of the *individual* human being against the *conventions* of courtly love; each is the result of developments peculiar to a specific story which happens to be treated according to the rules of courtly love. In brief, the poetry of courtly love is a predominantly masculine affair, with the concept of the woman used only as a crystallizing agent for the lover's conventional emotions.

In the *Temple of Glas*, on the contrary, Lydgate's preoccupation with the individual human being allows him to express what earlier poets of courtly love have failed even to suspect. He shows us the woman suffering, *not* because of events peculiar to the plot of the poem, but because she is an individual human being who bruises herself against a *convention* which expects her to pretend aloofness before her lover, while every emotional impulse in her urges immediate submission to the flesh: 'I most, of necessite,/Myn hertis lust outewards contrarie' (339–40).[42] A few lines later, Lydgate has her bitterly complain of the convention which necessarily denies her the consolation of sharing with someone else a sorrow which she is not supposed to endure in the first place:

> For thoughe I brenne with fervence and with hete
> Within myn hert, I mot complein of cold;
> And thurugh myn axcesse thoghe I sweltre and swete,
> Me to complein—God wot—I am not boold
> Unto no wight, nor a woord unfold
> Of al my peyne. (356–61)

Because of the size of some of the works considered and the multitude of references to women, the evidence presented here has necessarily been selective, but the very fact that it is possible to select such evidence supports the thesis that Lydgate's attitude toward individual human beings, far from being strictly mediaeval, was somewhat akin to that which we have been taught to seek in Renaissance humanism. If the evidence selected is as representative as I have tried to make it, it also suggests that here as in respect to classical antiquity Lydgate seems to have progressed intellectually toward the Renaissance. The earlier part of his poetic career reveals a supposedly mediaeval fondness for evaluating human beings according to preconceived notions about the category in which they were born; the later part shows a willingness to look upon each individual human being with something of the respect which the Renaissance has presumably taught us to consider the birthright of the paragon of animals.

Chapter Seven

THE NATION AND THE PRINCE

WHAT HAS BEEN SAID earlier about classical antiquity and the dignity of man must be repeated here about the common notion that nationalism is a characteristic of the Renaissance which neatly distinguishes that period from the Middle Ages: it is at best a very useful half-truth. Although the England of Elizabeth was more nationalistic than that of Stephen of Blois, nationalism did not suddenly appear the day the Queen ascended the throne. There can be little doubt that nationalism grew strong among the English in the wake of the Norman Conquest, and we find a bitter expression of the sentiment in the words of an anonymous chronicler's lament about the intrusion of French upon his native English: 'þurh þeos [i.e. Bede, Aelfric, and Alcuin] weren ilærde ure leoden on Englisc/ . . . . Nu beoþ oþre leoden þeo laereþ ure folc.'[1] It is common knowledge that Robert of Gloucester's *Chronicle*[2] and Layamon's *Brut*[3] contain likewise many nationalistic passages, and so do Barbour's *Bruce* and the poems of Laurence Minot. But then we must make a distinction between nationalism in the modern sense and the sentiment probably common to all ages and geographic locations that one's immediate compatriots are more trustworthy than the strangers who inhabit other lands and that one's home army is *ipso facto* more honourable than the enemy.[4] Though nationalism obviously existed during the Middle Ages, the form under which we think of it today did not become widespread until the end of the fourteenth century or the beginning of the fifteenth. We must not forget that in earlier times Hildebrand could feel free to take arms for his overlord Attila against his own compatriots in both the *Hildebrandslied* and the *Nibelungenlied*. With the progressive disintegration of the feudal system, however, people began to feel that they had common interests and were somehow bound together by their country, language, and ruler. This phenomenon, according to Sidney Painter, marked 'the beginning of what the historian calls nationalism'.[5]

That the sense of duty toward one's fatherland was spreading throughout western Europe during the early fifteenth century can be inferred from Alain Chartier's *Quadrilogue Invectif*, written in 1422, in which France is shown arguing with the three estates. She is not reminding them of their duty toward God or the King, but rather begging them to have mercy on her, their common mother.[6] Nationalism probably developed faster in England than on the Continent,[7] and Lydgate's position as the poet most patronized by the English rulers of the period made him particularly susceptible to its influence.

Moreover, nationalism developed in England somewhat earlier than the other attitudes which we have thus far associated with the Renaissance, and it seems to have already exercised a decided influence upon Lydgate at a time when the others were just beginning to make their mark. Whereas we have detected only timid traces of humanism in the *Troy Book*, we are struck by the violent nationalism which pervades the work from beginning to end. The legend of Troy was an ideal vehicle for the expression of nationalistic views. Since the Middle Ages held the conviction that the Trojans, through Aeneas's great-grandson Brutus, were the actual ancestors of the English people, a long poem about the rise and fall of Troy had somewhat the emotional appeal of a national epic. It is therefore not surprising that the Trojan ancestry of England should be mentioned early in the *Troy Book*:

> . . . cam Brute, so passyngly famus,
> After whom, yif I schal nat feyne,
> Whilom this lond called was Breteyne;

For he of geauntys thorugh his manhood wan
This noble yle, and it first began. (I, 832–6)

Thirty years later, in the opening lines of his *Kings of England Sithen William Conqueror*,[8] Lydgate will again name Brutus as the first ruler of England:

Froom tyme of Brute, auctours do specefye,
Two hundrid and fowr and twenty be succession
Kynges regned, til tym the monarchie
Devouht Alffrede took pocession. (1–4)

Nor does he ever express doubt concerning the historicity of the Trojan legend. In the prologue to the *Troy Book*, we read that the abduction of Helen and the subsequent destruction of Troy are facts whose authenticity has been attested by such authorities as Dares and Dictys:

But toforn alle, Dares Frigius
Wrote most trewly after that he fonde,
And Dytes eke of the Grekys lond. (Prologue, 310–12)

Because of his respect for history, Lydgate must report the facts as he finds them, but nothing compels him to like them or prevents him from interpreting them as he wishes. Accordingly, his Trojans must go down, ancestors of England though they be; but Homer is not permitted to get away with his praise of the Greek victors:

And al for [Homer] with Grekis was allied,
Therfor he was to hem favourable
In myche thing, which is nought commendable
Of hem that lyst to demen after ryght;
For in makyng, love hath lost his syght,
To yeve a pris wher noon is disserved;
Cupid is blynde, whos domys ben observyd
More after lust than after equite
Or after resoun how the trouthe was. (Prologue, 280–8)

Placed in juxtaposition, the two episodes most suggestive of the way in which nationalism affects Lydgate's treatment of his material are perhaps the death of Hector and that of Achilles. The death of Hector is presented as practically accidental. In preparation to looting the corpse of a fallen enemy, the Trojan prince has carelessly cast his shield behind his back, and he is so engrossed in his project that he fails to notice Achilles, who is thus enabled to slay him by surprise:

> This Achilles, cruel and venemous,
> Of hertly hate most malencolyous,
> Whiche covertly havynge hym beside,
> Whan that he saw Hector disarmyd ride,
> He hent a spere sharpe grounde and kene,
> And of ire in his hateful tene,
> Al unwarly, or Hector myght adverte—
> Alas the whyle!—he smote hym to the herte,
> Thorughoute the brest, that ded he fil doun
> Unto the erthe, this Troyan champion,
> Thorugh necligence only of his shelde. (III, 5389–99)

When, a few lines later, Lydgate begs for the inspiration to compose a lamentation worthy of Hector's fame, the deep sympathy with which the utterance is fraught movingly transcends the triteness so often attendant upon the topos of affected modesty:

> But now, allas! how shal I procede
> In the story, that for wo and drede
> Fele myn hond bothe tremble and quake?
> O worthi Hector, only for thi sake,
> Of thi deth I am so loth to write.
> O, who shal now help me to endyte,
> Or unto whom shal I clepe or calle?
> Certis to noon of the musis alle
> That by accorde singen ever in on
> Upon Pernasso, besiden Elycon,
> So angelik in her armonye. (III, 5423–33)

Whereas Hector is the hero, Achilles is definitely the villain of the affair. When, several thousand lines farther in the poem, the Greek warrior slays Hector's brother, Troilus, Lydgate finds occasion to abandon the text he is translating and berate the slayer for what he considers two most unworthy deeds:

> But, O allas! that evere it shulde falle
> A knyght to bene in herte so cruel
> Or of hatred so dispitous fel. (IV, 2780–2)

He then proceeds to upbraid Homer for having condoned Achilles' victories over the two brothers:

> O thou, Omer, for shame be now red,
> And be astonyd, that haldest thi silfe so wyse,
> On Achilles to setten swiche a pris!
> In thi bokes for his chivalrie
> Above echon dost hym magnyfye,
> That was so sleighty and so ful of fraud!
> Whi yevest thou hym so highe a pris and laude? (IV, 2784–90)

After a brief rehearsal of Achilles' treachery, he again addresses Homer with an adjuration to reform:

> Wherfor, Omer, preise hym now no more.
> Lat nat his pris thi rial boke difface,
> But in all haste his renoun oute arace;
> For his name whan I here nevene,
> Verrailly up into the hevene,
> As semeth me, infect is the eyr,
> The sown therof so foule is and unfair! (IV, 2834–40)

Before finally dropping the matter, he warns us a last time that Homer's praise of Achilles 'Entriked is with fraude and with fallas' (III, 2835).

Lydgate's reaction at the slaying of Achilles is radically different. Queen Hecuba, we are told, asks the Greek warrior to a temple under the pretext of discussing his possible marriage to one of her daughters. No sooner have he and a single companion reached the appointed place than she has them set upon by Paris and twenty Trojans who hew them to pieces despite their heroic defence. By common ethical standards the Queen's action constitutes as treacherous a murder as one can imagine. Yet Lydgate, whose wrath at the slaying of Hector could not be appeased, dismisses this murder as something done 'rightfully, of resoun as it sit' (III, 3195). When Achilles' body is thrown to the dogs, he placidly concludes that such is the end of 'fals deceit compassid by envie' (III, 3212). The truth is simply that Hecuba, as direct ancestor of the English nation, can do nothing wrong, while her enemies can do nothing right; and Lydgate thus opens himself unwittingly to the same charge of partiality which he so often levels at Homer.

Lydgate never swerves from the conviction that the Trojan ancestors of the English nation fell only because of Antenor's treachery (IV, 5216 ff.), Calchas' desertion (IV, 6026 ff.), and Mars' malice (IV, 4453, 4470, 4475). He is particularly bitter toward the god, whom he considers the engineer behind the whole disaster (IV, 6026 ff.), and whom he curses roundly:

> . . . for thi malys on Troy the cite,
> So wolde God I koude chide aright
> That hath on hem kyd thi felle myght,
> Of thi rancour hooly the outtrance. (VI, 4484–7)

The assumption underlying the narrative of the *Troy Book* is exactly the same as that which John de Stogomber, in George Bernard Shaw's *Saint Joan*, makes when he indignantly exclaims, 'We were not fairly beaten, my lord. No Englishman is ever fairly beaten',[9] and we should not be surprised to hear Lydgate end his work on a similar note.[10]

As we read the apostrophe to Mars we should keep in mind that, despite the dashing and valiant attempts of Henry V, the general state of the conflict between England and France was giving Lydgate no cause to be favourably disposed toward the God of War. His own words, almost at the end of the poem, suggest as much:

> And thanne I hope the tyme fortunat
> Of the olde worlde called aureate
> Resorte shal by influence of grace
> That cruel Mars shal no more manace
> With his lokis furious and wood
> By false aspectus for to shede blood
> Atwene the folkes of this rewmys tweyne
> Which every wyght oughte to compleyne. (V, 3399–3406)

Because the *Troy Book* tells the story of the legendary ancestors of England, it affords Lydgate innumerable occasions to vent his nationalism. The *Fall of Princes*, however, is the work in which we find the clearest instance of his nationalistic feelings. When Boccaccio relates how King John of France was deprived of his kingdom by 'anglis, inertissimis adque pauidis et nullius valoris hominibus'—that is to say, by Englishmen, the laziest and most fearful of worthless men—Laurent de Premierfait translates accurately as 'des anglois, hommes faillis et vains et de nulle valeur'.[11] This is not the sort of statement which we may expect a patriotic Englishman to accept, and Lydgate adapts it accordingly to suit his own opinion of his compatriots:

> The same tyme in Brutis Albioun
> Ther floured in soth noblesse of chevalrie,
> Hihe prowesse, and prudent pollicie—
> Mars and Mercurie above each nacioun
> Governed that tyme Brutis Albioun. (IX, 3150–4)

Nor can he resist the impulse of his patriotic indignation, and without any further pretence at staying with his text he gives Boccaccio a fierce tongue-lashing for his impertinence:

> For to hyndre the famous chevalrie
> Of Inglisshmen, ful narwe he gan hym thynke,
> Lefft spere and sheelde, fauht with penne and inke.
>
> Thouh seide Bochas floured in poetrie,
> His parcial writyng gaf no mortal wounde;
> Kauhte a quarel in his malencolie,
> Which to his shame did afterward rebounde,
> In conclusion, lik as it was founde,
> Ageyn King John a quarel gan to make,
> Cause that he wolde of Inglisshmen be take.
> Heeld hem but smal of reputacioun,
> In his report man may his writing see;
> His fantasie nor his oppynioun
> Stood in that caas of noon auctorite:
> Ther kyng was take; ther knihtis dide flee;
> Where was Bochas to help at such a neede?
> Sauff with his penne he made no man to bleede.
> (IX, 3166–82)

The same spirit is present in the *Debate of the Horse, Sheep, and Goose*,[12] probably composed between 1437 and 1440. The topic is supposedly a debate in which the three animals of the title attempt to decide which of them is the most useful to mankind. Within this frame Lydgate contrives to suggest the superiority of England over the rest of the world. Thus, the account which the goose gives of himself is little more than a pretext to extol the warlike qualities of Englishmen and the effectiveness of their long bow:

> Trough al the lond of Brutis Albion
> For fetherid arwes, as I reherse can,
> Goos is the best as in comparisonn,
> Except fetheris of pekok or of swan:
> Bi bowe and arwis sith the werr began,
> Have Ynglysshmen, as it is red in story,
> On her enmyes had many gret victory. (211–17)

Likewise, the sheep's answer to the goose principally asserts the superiority of English wool over all others:

> Alle naciouns afferme up to the fulle,
> In al the world ther is no bettir wolle. (356–7)

We may be amused at Lydgate when his nationalism takes the form of a versified encomium of English wool or grossly blinds him to the treachery of the Trojan queen, but his more inspired moments do not deserve the usual contempt. His reply to Boccaccio's belittling of English chivalry may disappoint the modern reader who vainly searches it for the spirit of Chaucer, but we need not stretch our sensitivities very far to discover that the sentiments expressed here are quite similar to those which we rightfully admire when John of Gaunt delivers them in Shakespeare's *Richard II*. To both Shakespeare and Lydgate, England *is* 'This precious stone set in the silver sea' (II, 1, 46).

I have said earlier in this chapter that the difference between the nationalism of the Middle Ages and that of subsequent times is not so clear as we often assume. In English vernacular literature not avowedly concerned with immediate local history, the key may perhaps—but only perhaps—be found in the willingness of the Renaissance and later periods to disseminate the influence of nationalism into enquiries not avowedly concerned with this subject. For instance, whereas 'the very mediaeval Chaucer',[122] as Utley has called him, readily bows to Dante and Petrarch, Dryden enters the battle between Ancients and Moderns not only on the latter's side but with an argument in favour of his immediate compatriots. In other words, the Renaissance seems to have been somewhat more eager than the Middle Ages to let its nationalistic feelings permeate various subjects and to make other subjects an excuse for expressing that nationalism; and outright expressions of nationalism seem to have been rather more intense than in earlier centuries.[13] Thus Lydgate's departure from Boccaccio when the latter belittles the English nation does not necessarily clash with the attitude of his predecessors,[14] and the fact is that Duke Humphrey might not have relished an exact English rendering of the Italian's views. On the other hand, the additional remonstration and the intensity thereof also remind us of his followers; and his making a debate between a horse, a goose, and a sheep an excuse for asserting the superiority of England over the rest of the world is frankly nationalism for its own sake. It would be foolish to assert that the nationalistic elements discussed above make Lydgate a sort of Renaissance poet ahead of his own time, but it is by no means so foolish to say that they make it difficult to go on considering him as strictly illustrative of the mediaeval mind in this respect.

With the emergence of nationalism on a large scale, the Renaissance naturally turned its attention to the behaviour of those who controlled the fate of the nation. To understand how that period looked at the relationship between the ruler's behaviour and national welfare, it is sufficient to open Shakespeare's *Hamlet* and listen to Rosenkrantz's definition of a king:

> It is a massy wheel,
> Fix'd on the summit of the highest mount,
> To whose huge spokes ten thousand lesser things
> Are mortis'd and adjoin'd; which, when it falls,
> Each small annexment, petty consequence,
> Attends the boisterous ruin. (III, iii, 17–22)

With such an assumption as a motivating force, it is normal that serious writers should reveal unprecedented interest in the conduct of the Prince and his entourage, and the results of their concern are found in such works as Machiavelli's *Prince*, Castiglione's *Courtier*, and Elyot's *Governor*.

Here again a word of caution is necessary, for we need only turn to John of Salisbury's *Policraticus*, Dante's *Monarchia*, or the *De Regimine Principum*, of which parts are attributed to St.

Thomas Aquinas and others to Ptolemy of Lucca, to realize that the Middle Ages were very much concerned with the nature and behaviour of the prince and his relation to national welfare. In this respect as in the case of nationalism, the difference between the Middle Ages and the Renaissance may well lie in the context and dissemination of the materials. Whereas Rosenkrantz's statement in *Hamlet* occurs in a play and is intended for the benefit of anyone who cares to attend a performance—and this presumably means the illiterate as well as the learned—the lessons of the *Policraticus*, the *Monarchia*, and the *De Regimine Principum* are addressed specifically to a lettered audience concerned with the workings of the body politic. Whereas *The Prince*, *The Courtier*, and *The Governor* are respectively within reach of anyone who can read Italian or English, the mediaeval treatises cited above assume the reader's knowledge of Latin, as does Gower's *Vox Clamantis*. But the mediaeval concern for the behaviour of rulers is not expressed exclusively in Latin treatises, and we find it in the vernacular long before the Renaissance, in fact long before the fifteenth century. In English *Piers the Plowman* and *Robert of Sicily* immediately come to mind. The former, however, is the expression of immediate grievances rather than of a methodical political philosophy; and the latter is clearly an *exemplum* designed to illustrate with a simple anecdote the lesson that kings ought to respect the clergy. In general mediaeval writers do not seem to have assumed that government and the education of rulers was the concern of their readers at large.

The secular works of Lydgate reflect a keen and growing concern for the behaviour of rulers. The *Troy Book* already contains occasional instances of advice to rulers, but these are so frankly intended to foster the welfare of the Prince as a person rather than as a symbol of the nation[15] that they may not readily serve as evidence for the present argument. With his very next major work, however, he seems to have become conscious of the ruler's duty toward the nation as well as toward himself, for the *Siege of Thebes* is principally designed to formulate and illustrate the ideal comportment of the prince. The means whereby the poet accomplishes his design will be discussed in the next chapter.

The prose *Serpent of Division,* probably written in 1422,[16] retells the story of the war between Caesar and Pompey and offers it to rulers as an illustration of the catastrophic results of ambition which they must eschew not only for their own sake but especially for the sake of the nation as a whole. The verse envoy is categorical on this point:

> This litill prose declarith in figure
> The grete damage and distruccion,
> That whilome fill, bi fatell aventure,
> Unto Rome, the myghti riall towne,
> Caused onely bi false devision
> Amonge hem selfe, the storie tellith this,
> Thorowe covetise and veyne ambicion
> Of Pompey and Cesar Julius.
>
> Criste hymselfe recordith in scripture
> That every londe and every region
> Whiche is devided may no while endure,
> But turne in haste to desolacion;
> For whiche, ye lordes and prynces of renowne,
> So wyse, so manly, and so vertuous,
> Maketh a merowre toforne in youre resoun
> Of Pompey and Cesar Julius. (p. 66)

Eight years later in a *Ballade to King Henry VI Upon His Coronation,* Lydgate will again warn his sovereign to 'eschuwe werre and debate', to be always equitable and merciful, and never to neglect the welfare of the poor.[17]

The title *De Casibus Virorum Illustrium* indicates that Boccaccio's intention in writing that work was to illustrate the transitoriness of worldly power, and the three titles of Laurent de Premierfait's translation—*De la Ruyne des Nobles Hommes et Femmes, Des Cas et Ruyne des Nobles Hommes et Femmes,* and *Des Nobles Malheureux*—reveal no change in purpose in the French translation.[18] Indeed, the emphasis in both the Latin and the French is on the dire effects of Fortune upon men. The title under which modern scholars know the English version is that by which Lydgate himself refers to Boccaccio's as he sets out to translate it: 'And John Bochas wrot . . ./The fall of prynces' (I, 269–70). The change from the Latin and the French to the English is significant;

in substituting the word 'princes' for the words 'illustrious men' or 'noble men' which one would expect, Lydgate calls our attention to the importance of rulers and thus emphasizes at the start the central purpose of his own work.

Nor is the change of title merely a pious manifesto for the benefit of Humphrey of Gloucester. On the contrary, Lydgate keeps his initial promise throughout the work. For instance, he does not hesitate to depart from Laurent in order to assert the necessity that 'noble prynces be governed by resoun' (II, 56), or to exhort rulers to enact laws to keep the nation at peace:

Wherfor, ye pryncis, doth sum lawe ordeyne,
Withynne your boundis thre vices to restreyne:

The vice off sclaundre, moordre, and poisoun.
Wherever these thre haven aqueyntaunce,
Thei brynge in sorwe and desolacioun,
Put at a preeff be newe remembraunce
Off falsheed used under fair cuntenaunce.
Wherfor, ye pryncis, doth your besi peyne,
Withynne your boundis these vices to restreyne. (III, 902–10)

With the next statement, incidentally, he succeeds in giving simultaneous expression to both his concern for the comportment of princes and his nationalism:

God diffende this noble regioun
With these thre vices to have alliaunce

. . . . .

Wherfor, ye pryncis, doth a lawe ordeyne
To punshe ther malice. (III, 911–17)

The *Fall of Princes* makes repeated attempts at defining the nature of true regality, to which it refers as something that comes only as a result of virtuous conduct.[19] Even though the poem was written at the request of a great nobleman, Lydgate is here bringing within reach of the general reading public a political theory which the mediaeval John of Salisbury had reserved for the learned[20] and which is not untypical of the Renaissance.[21] Carried to its logical and very unmediaeval extreme, it may lead a nation to behead its king because he has proved unworthy of his tenure;[22] in the normal course of events it merely leads to contempt for the means whereby hereditary titles of nobility are normally acquired, and we read words to this effect in the poem:

> Thus erthli princis, with al ther pompous fame,
> Which thoruh the world yiveth so gret a soun,
> Of slauhtre and moordre thei tooke first ther name,
> Bi fals ravyne and extorsioun
> Clamb up so first do domynacioun,
> Brennyng of contres, conquest bi violence
> Sette hem in chaieres of worldli excellence. (VI, 2457–64)

This is a powerful statement, and the extent to which it is Lydgate's own may easily be ascertained by comparison with its milder and much more cautious counterpart in Laurent's text: 'ilz [i.e. the titled lords] sont par la souffrance de dieu devenus seigneurs du monde par occisions dhommes, par larcin de pays, et par mil autres violences'.[23]

At this point we have at our disposal the premises for a weak but tempting syllogistic argument: if regality is the result of virtuous conduct, and if hereditary titles are utterly meaningless, then anyone with the required moral qualities may become a true king. The conclusion to this syllogism is formulated in the *Fall of Princes*:

> But in contrarie, who list hymsilf to knowe
> And is be grace enclyned to meeknesse,
> Thouh he from povert in streihtnesse brouht up lowe
> And is be vertu reised to worthynesse,
> With sceptre of pes and swerd of rihtwisnesse
> Indifferentli his doomys demenyng—
> Such oon is able to be cleped a kyng. (V, 2831–7)

This statement, which carries over to the next stanza, concludes the story of the tyrant Zebina. The English, which emphasizes the ideal nature of the ruler, significantly leaves out two passages present in the French: one is a brief introductory note on Fortune's deplorable habit of toying with those who rise in status; the other is a diatribe against the 'vilz hommes et varletz eslevez en haulte dignitez' (p. 245)—the low-born men and wretches who rise to high dignity.

The foregoing observations show that toward the end of his

career Lydgate was deeply concerned with the ideal nature of the Prince; they do not, however, suggest that he advocated picking any likely upstart for a ruler regardless of his family background and training. The fifteenth century had seen too much of the cruelty, extravagance, and greed of the newly rich to wish them more power than they had already acquired,[24] and the *Fall of Princes* specifically warns against the evils that may befall the nation 'Whan beggers rise to domynacion' (II, 3025).

As Lydgate grew older his increasing interest in the nature of kingship may be said to have partially alienated him from the ways of thinking of the Middle Ages and brought him nearer to those of the Renaissance. Thus, it is fitting that his very last work should have been devoted exclusively to the guidance of the King. The *Secrees of Old Philisoffres*, his translation from the very mediaeval *Secreta Secretorum* which death prevented him from completing,[25] is expressly written for the benefit of 'prudent prynces most digne of reverence' (33). The prologue expresses the wish that God will confirm the King in his intention to rule England 'by polityk lyving' (3), and particularly 'in al vertu to sette his governaunce' (8). By the time death put an end to his work, Lydgate had not proceeded far beyond giving kings advice of purely personal and practical import about the proper way to dress, the importance of selecting a competent physician, and similar trivial matters. He could not, however, have been unaware that later sections of the *Secreta Secretorum* treated the relationship between the King and the nation,[26] and that his translation would make the lesson of the Latin available to anyone who could read English.

That the lesson in the *Secrees of Old Philisoffres* was still meaningful to the early English Renaissance is a point hardly worth arguing, for Richard Pynson printed it in 1511 under the title of *The Governaunce of Kynges and Prynces*.[27] Of more importance to the present argument is the popularity until the early seventeenth century of *The Mirror for Magistrates*, the Renaissance continuation of the *Fall of Princes*. Farnham is definite on this point where he reminds us that 'Lydgate's *Fall of Princes* had maintained secure popularity through the fifteenth century and into the sixteenth' and that the *Mirror* was 'conceived merely as an appendage . . . to be used as an extension of Lydgate's classic';[28] and he emphasizes the fact that the *Mirror* 'was enormously prolific in editions and imitations until 1610'.[29] The importance of these observations is that, beyond suggesting the Renaissance popularity of Lydgate's views on the nature of regality and its relationship to national welfare, they suggest that they were congenial enough to the Renaissance mind to warrant their extension beyond the chronological conclusion of the *Fall of Princes*. The possibility may probably receive various explanations, but it adds evidence to my contention that we ought not to accept uncritically the common notion that Lydgate's poetry was exclusively mediaeval in its appeal.

Chapter Eight

THE STORY OF THEBES

THE THREE most important secular works of Lydgate are the *Troy Book*, the *Siege of Thebes*, and the *Fall of Princes*. Their composition occupied a considerable portion of his life;[1] they were immensely popular with their own age as well as with the Elizabethans; two of them are among the longest poems of all times; all three have kept generations of scholars busy tracing sources and ferreting out the influence of Chaucer; and they have afforded innumerable critics many a self-gratifying witticism at the expense of their author. Thus far my investigation has neglected the *Siege of Thebes* in favour of the other two, because the nearly thirty years between the undertaking of one and the completion of the other make them respectively illustrative of Lydgate's intellectual position toward the beginning and toward the end of his most active period. In addition, the changes revealed by comparing these two works were most certainly progressive, so that they might not prove so easy to detect in works written over a briefer period. Having defined these changes in the preceding chapters, we may now turn to the *Siege of Thebes* and try to determine its place in the course of its author's intellectual evolution. Because the poem was composed about 1421,[2] the examination will tell us something concerning his position after the completion of the mediaeval *Troy Book* and before the beginning of the somewhat humanistic *Fall of Princes*.

In one respect the *Siege of Thebes* may be considered peculiarly representative of its author's ways of thinking: it is the only major secular work of Lydgate to have been composed outside the patronage system. I have said earlier that the poem was possibly intended to be read by Henry V, and we shall see that its lesson is addressed to the King; but there is not the remotest evidence to suggest that Henry ever asked for it. Thus the choice of the subject must be Lydgate's own, and whatever we read in the poem must be here because the poet wanted it here rather than because he was complying with a patron's request.

The *Siege of Thebes* is further representative of its author in two other ways. In the first place, it is not a translation in the modern sense, but rather an exceptionally free and elaborate adaptation of a mediocre French prose romance. Since Lydgate seems to have felt no responsibility toward the French beyond that of using it as a basis for his own story, the English text may be considered a sample of his own creativity. In the second place, it is the only attempt at narrating the entire Theban legend in English. We know that while composing the *Troy Book* Lydgate occasionally took his cue from the *Gest Hystoriale of the Destruction of Troy*,[3] and the chances are that he consulted Chaucer's *Monk's Tale* while working on the *Fall of Princes*,[4] even though the two works have only the vaguest outline in common. Such cannot be the case with the *Siege of Thebes*, since no English precursor existed to serve as a model. Of course, he was undoubtedly familiar with Chaucer's references to the story of Thebes, particularly those in the *Knight's Tale*, *Troilus and Criseyde*, and *Anelida and Arcite*; but these are much too sketchy and isolated to serve as models for a poem of 4,716 lines, and they have contributed nothing beyond the forms selected for the names of several characters.[5] Since Lydgate presented his poem as an addition to the *Canterbury Tales*, he naturally used Chaucer now and then,[6] but his borrowing was free from the tyranny of a specific model whose example must be constantly followed.

Since the composition of the *Siege of Thebes* was apparently Lydgate's own idea, we may well wonder about his reasons for selecting this particular subject. The answer, I believe, can be easily guessed. With the completion of his *Troy Book* in 1420, Lydgate had just finished devoting eight years to a subject which the mediaeval literary mind almost invariably associated with the legend of Thebes. The Continental writers of the thirteenth and fourteenth centuries seldom mention Troy without also mentioning Thebes; the two stories are often narrated as one continuous unit; and an overwhelming majority of the French redactions of the story of Troy are bound together with redactions of the story of Thebes, usually in immediate juxtaposition.[7] Lydgate must have been aware of the artificial but powerful bond which united the two stories, for he felt the need of mentioning the legend of Thebes at the outset of the *Troy Book* (prologue, 266 ff.) and of returning to it twice in the course of the narrative (IV, 3013 and 3023). If we accept Henry Noble MacCracken's contention that the *Troy Book* enjoyed an immediately favourable reception,[8] then we have an answer to our query: nothing could be more natural for Lydgate than to wish to go on with the traditional companion of the subject that had just brought him fame, and the motivation was certainly not lessened by the consciousness that his poem would be the only English version of an extremely famous legend.

There is an additional reason why the story of Thebes may have attracted Lydgate. As already noted, his poem is conspicuous for the amount of advice it offers concerning the conduct of royalty. Without counting subtle hints which may not have been consciously intended as guidance for anybody in particular one finds twenty-two instances of advice to royalty, or 555 lines out of a total 4,716. Three hundred and nineteen of these consist of suggestions and admonitions either offered by Lydgate himself or spoken by characters in the poem, but obviously aimed at the reader rather than at the other characters. The remaining 236 lines form an intrinsic part of the plot but are clearly written with the reader's edification in mind, for they usually lead to discussions of the evils and blessings to which kingship is heir. Because the most immediate problem facing England during the first quarter of the fifteenth century was the war with France, the story of the war between Thebes and Argos not only offered countless opportunities for pointedly relevant advice on the conduct of royalty in time of war, but could also be fashioned into an oversized exemplum to be foisted upon the dashing and reckless young King who had led the English at Agincourt. In this respect it is interesting that the only version of the story explicitly named in Lydgate's poem is the *Thebaid* of Statius, which offers two outstanding instances of advice to royalty.[9] Thus in 1420–1, Lydgate's concern with the conduct of princes had already grown strong enough to prove possibly instrumental in the selection of his subject-matter.

The decision to present the *Siege of Thebes* as an addition to the *Canterbury Tales* likewise calls for some explanation. As Erdmann suggests, Chaucer's failure to complete his own announced scheme had provided tempting room for additions by subsequent poets,[10] and the presence of the *Tale of Beryn* and John Lane's continuation of the *Squire's Tale* in 1616 tells us that the temptation was not always resisted. But the observation that the inducement was there does not account for the fact that Lydgate himself reacted to it and that he chose the legend of Thebes for the subject of his addition. After all, he could as well have decided to complete the *Cook's Tale* if the spirit had moved him. Because only Lydgate himself could tell us what really promoted his decision, the explanation which follows is necessarily tentative; the key to it is a brief passage in the final section of the *Troy Book*:

> For almost wery, feint and waike inow
> Be the bestes and oxes of my plow,
> The longe day ageyn the hil to wende.
> But almost now at the londes ende
> Of Troy Book, ficche I wil a stake. (V, 2927–31)

The Knight of the *Canterbury Tales* makes an identical reference to weary oxen at the end of his summary of Queen Hippolyta's story:

> I have, God woot, a large feeld to ere,
> And wayke been the oxen in my plough. (886–7)

Considering that the similarity between the two statements is not only in the wording but also in the circumstances under which both are spoken, we cannot readily dismiss it as accidental. Furthermore, we must assume Lydgate to have known that the *Knight's Tale* was the only English poem to take two of its principal characters, as well as much of its material, from the Theban legend. Since the statement he borrows from Chaucer is recorded fewer than eight hundred lines from the conclusion of the *Troy Book*, he must have written it down at a time when he was already considering a poem about Thebes. It is not at all improbable that the idea occurred to him then to present his own projected work as a companion piece to the *Knight's Tale*. At least we may be sure that the idea was not an afterthought subsequent to the completion of the *Siege of Thebes*, for the poem contains six allusions to the scheme of the Canterbury Pilgrimage, and these are distributed throughout the narrative.[11]

Writing his own poem as an addition to the *Canterbury Tales* must have presented at least a threefold attraction for Lydgate. First, his poem could thus be regarded as the same sort of tribute to Chaucer which modern scholars are wont to pay their retired or deceased elders in the form of a *Festschrift*.[12] Second, the name of Chaucer would give the poem the same prestige which the name of Guido delle Colonne had given the *Troy Book* and the name of Giovanni Boccaccio would eventually give the *Fall of Princes*. Third, the scheme would allow the poet to put a new twist on his favourite theme of affected modesty. Besides protesting his own inadequacies, he could have the well-known and uninhibited Host of the *Canterbury Tales* boisterously address him as an inconsequential idiot. In the prologue to the *Siege of Thebes*, Lydgate imagines himself accidentally entering the inn where Chaucer's Pilgrims are staying in Canterbury. His appearance is so ridiculously lamentable that the Host cannot resist the impulse of addressing him with a mixture of contempt and good humour:

> Daun Pers,
> Daun Domynyk, Dan Godfrey, or Clement,
> Ye be welcom newly into Kent,
> Thogh youre bridel have neither boos ne belle;
> Besechinge you that ye wil me telle
> First youre name, and of what contre
> Withoute more shortely that ye be,
> That loke so pale, al devoyde of blood,
> Upon youre hede a wonder thredbar hood,
> Wel araied for to ride late. (82–91)

The Host then invites the meek and embarrassed Lydgate to join the Pilgrims at the dinner table and ride back to London with them on the morrow; he then urges him to take a draught of nutty ale to help him snore, and boisterously advises him to break wind in order to avoid the colic:

> Strong notty ale wol make you to route;
> Tak a pylow that ye lye not lowe.
> Yif nede be, spare not to blowe!
> To holde wynde, be myn opynyoun,
> Wil engendre collikes passioun. (110–13)

After several more remarks in the same vein, he enjoins the victim of his jocularity to have a gay tale wherewith to entertain the Pilgrims the next morning:

> What! look up, Monk, for, by kokkis blood,
> Thow shalt be mery, whoso that sey nay.
> For tomorowe, anoon as it is day
> And that it gynne in the est to dawe,
> Thow shalt be bounde . . .
>
> To telle a tale pleynly as thei konne,
> Whan I assigne and se tyme opportune. (126–39)

Nor does he forget his injunction to Lydgate, and the Pilgrims are no sooner on their way to London than he reiterates it with renewed gusto and very much in the same peremptory tone:

> Come forth, Daun John be your Cristene name,
> And lat us make some manere myrth or play!
>
> . . . . .
>
> Gynne some tale of myrth or of gladnesse,
> And nodde not with thyn hevy bekke!
> Telle us some thyng that draweth to effecte
> Only of joye. Make no lenger lette! (160–71)

This introduction allows the poet to proceed with his narration without laying himself open to the charge of presumption:

> And when I saugh it wolde be no bette,
> I obeyed unto his biddynge,
> So as the lawe me bonde in al thinge;
> And as I coude, with a pale cheere,
> My tale I gan anon, as ye shal here. (172–6)

With these words, he is in effect complying with Cicero's precept that orators should show submissiveness and humility, and he unwittingly follows the example of Pliny, who would have us believe he collected his own letters only because he was ordered to do so. The coincidence is relevant to the present argument because Curtius has advanced the theory that the statements of Cicero and Pliny are at the origin of the topos of affected modesty.[13]

The device discussed above is not the only instance in the poem where Lydgate conforms to the literary practices of the mediaeval tradition. We have already noted that he begins the narrative with an apology for his dullness of wit.[14] As is only proper with a retelling of the Theban legend written as an addition to the *Canterbury Tales*, he includes an encomium of Chaucer in the prologue (38 ff.) and refers to the *Knight's Tale* a few lines before the end (4501 ff.). He likewise practises the device of *pauca e multis*, as, for example, when he mentions his eagerness not to tax the reader's patience as the principal reason for cutting short a description of two beautiful maidens:

> But sothly I have leyser non nor space
> To reherce and put in remembraunce
> Hooly the maner of her daliaunce;
> It were to longe for you to abide. (1476–9)

A little later he apologizes for giving only a brief description of a sumptuous banquet: 'For lak of tyme I lat it overslyde' (1565). Toward the end of the poem he offers similar apologies for giving us only a sample of the Argive women's lamentation for the warriors who fall before Thebes:

> And yif I shulde by and by descryve
> Ther tendre wepyng and ther wooful sownys,
> Her complayntys and lamentacions,
> Her ofte swounyng with facys ded and pale,
> Therof I myghte make a newe tale
> Almost a day you to occupye. (4420–5)

Lydgate reveals in yet another way his attachment to the rhetorical devices of the Middle Ages. Although nature plays an insignificant part in the *Siege of Thebes*, no reader is likely to forget the storm which surprises Oedipus's son Polynices on his way from Thebes to Argos:

> And sodeynly the se began to rore,
> Wynde and tempest hidously tarise.
> The reyn doune bete in ful grisly wise,
> That man and beest therof were adrad
> And negh for fere gan to wexe mad,
> As it sempte by the wooful sownes
> Of tygres, beres, boores, and lyounes,
> Which for refut, hemsilve for to save,
> Everich in hast drogh unto his cave. (1174–82)

The notion of a Greek forest inhabited by lions and tigers seems ridiculous to us, and it would probably have seemed equally ridiculous to Lydgate if he had taken his own statement at face value. Both he and his audience, however, must have looked upon the mention of exotic fauna as nothing more realistic than a commonplace of mediaeval rhetoric; lions appear in Peter of Pisa, in Alcuin, in the *Nibelungenlied*, and in many other places where their presence is quite unwarranted according to the laws of nature. Curtius, who remarks that 'the French epic swarms with lions',[15] has shown that they are pure stylization without the remotest pretence to represent reality.

Like the other works of Lydgate which we have examined thus far, the *Siege of Thebes* draws its narrative devices largely from the mediaeval tradition. The same thing may not be said of the lesson it teaches. The nature and intensity of that lesson may best be understood through occasional comparisons with the French text which served as a basis for the English poem. Lydgate has unfortunately neglected to identify that document more specifically than as his 'auctour' (199, 877, 1266), so that we have to rely on literary historians who have shown that it must have been a prose redaction of the Old-French *Roman de Thebes* similar in all but a few details to the *Roman de Edipus*.[16]

The outline of the French text may be divided in two. The first and shorter section tells the story of Oedipus. We learn that he was born in Thebes to King Laius and Queen Jocasta. Because of adverse oracles, his father orders him killed and exposed, but the executioners merely hang him from a tree by holes pierced in his feet and subsequently tell Jocasta that they have killed him. Oedipus is saved by hunters and adopted by King Polybus of Arcadia. After a brief account of the founding of Thebes, the redactor tells how Oedipus eventually learns of his adoption and is sent to Thebes by an oracle which assures him he will find his father there. In the course of his journey he meets King Laius, whom he accidentally kills in a joust. He then solves the Sphinx's riddle, with the result that he is elected King of Thebes and made to marry Jocasta. Many years later, after Jocasta has given birth to two sons and two daughters, she accidentally recognizes the scars on his feet and reveals to him the incestuous nature of their marriage. In horror, Oedipus pulls out his eyeballs and lets his scornful sons push him into a pit where he dies of sorrow.

The second and longer section tells how Oedipus's sons, Eteocles and Polynices, struggle with each other for the throne of Thebes and finally agree to reign by turn for a year at a time. Because he is the elder, Eteocles is crowned first. Polynices goes off in temporary exile and, after an arduous journey, reaches at midnight the city of Argos, governed by the good King Adrastus. He dismounts in silence and goes to sleep under a porch, where he is soon awakened by the arrival of a Calydonian prince named Tydeus, who asks to share the shelter. Polynices refuses the request and insists upon fighting the new-comer, thus waking up Adrastus, who enters the scene to separate the combatants. In the morning Adrastus succeeds in reconciling the two knights and, in answer to a dream, gives them his two daughters in marriage. A year passes, and Polynices begins thinking about returning to Thebes to claim the throne. Tydeus takes his message to Eteocles, who refuses to surrender the city and has the messenger ambushed on the way back to Argos. Tydeus survives, but his misadventure prompts Adrastus to take an expedition to Thebes. After a lengthy siege, Polynices and Eteocles kill each other in single combat, and their uncle Creon takes over the government and defence of the city. The besieging army is nearly annihilated when the Duke of Athens happens by on his way to punish a rebel vassal. Angered by Creon's refusal to let the dead Argives be buried, he storms the city and burns it to the ground. Adrastus returns to Argos, where death soon overtakes him. The poor people of Thebes eventually rebuild their city.

The English poem is formally divided into a prologue and three sections dealing respectively with the story of Oedipus, the exile of Polynices, and the Argive expedition against Thebes. The third section ends with a praise of peace and a prayer to Christ. If we omit the final statement about the rebuilding of Thebes, the outline of the *Roman de Edipus* suits the *Siege of Thebes* equally well. Here, however, ends the similarity between the two works; in all other respects they are separated by the immeasurable gap that lies between childish prose written to no lofty purpose and competent poetry composed with a philosophical intent. Lydgate departs from his original in five principal ways: he rectifies the often defective logic of the French; he presents classical antiquity in a much more appealing light; he formulates a lesson for the conduct of rulers; he turns the ancient legend into an English nationalistic narrative; and he creates in the person of Tydeus a hero for the story.

Lydgate's concern for the logical presentation of his material is evident both in the organization of the narrative and in the treatment of the details. The most cursory examination of the first section of the *Roman de Edipus* reveals two faults in organization and two inconsistencies: (1) the account of the founding of Thebes comes after the narrative has already shifted away from that city, thus awkwardly interrupting the story of Oedipus's youth; (2) when Jocasta discovers the fatal scars the redactor reminds us of the circumstances under which they were acquired and immediately allows her to repeat precisely the same story for Oedipus's benefit; (3) although Oedipus explicitly receives his name from King Polybus, the name is used in the narrative before the two ever meet; and (4) although the executioners explicitly inform the Queen that they have killed her infant, we are told at the end of the first section that she recognizes the scars because they had reported to her how they left him hanging from a tree.

None of these defects appears in the *Siege of Thebes*. Here the account of the founding of Thebes, which would begin on line 467 if Lydgate adhered to the French, begins on line 184, thus coming logically between the end of the prologue and the first mention of King Laius. The story of the exposed child is told only once, when Jocasta informs Oedipus of the incestuous nature of their relationship (908). The name of Oedipus is never used until King Polybus has decided upon it (452),[17] and the executioners' report to Jocasta is entirely left out, with the result that her version of the story can no longer conflict with theirs.[18]

The episodes of the slaying of King Laius and the encounter with the Sphinx lend themselves to the same kind of observations. In the French, Oedipus on his way to Thebes stops at a castle where he takes part in a tourney during which he accidentally kills King Laius. After a befitting display of grief, Laius's followers take his body back to Thebes, where Jocasta has it cremated. Only then do we read about Oedipus finally leaving the scene of the slaying (f. Aiiii *recto-verso*). Even though no one has seen the accident actually happen and Oedipus makes no effort to reveal his part in it, his tarrying seems ridiculously illogical if we think of the treatment normally awaiting a regicide if he were caught. Lydgate, on the contrary, mentions neither the mourning nor the cremation until he has told us, 'Edyppus in hast gan hym withdrawe' (566).

In its account of the events that brought about the meeting with the Sphinx, the French text relates that, upon leaving the castle where he had unwittingly killed his own father, Oedipus decided to avoid the common road and proceed toward Thebes by a roundabout path (f. Aiiii *verso*). There are only two logical ways of explaining his knowledge of such a path: either he was thoroughly familiar with the region, or he had made enquiries from the natives. In either case, he would have known that the path led straight to the hideout of a monster whose ferocity was famous enough to keep the entire country in awe (*ibid.*).[19] Yet the encounter with the Sphinx comes as a complete surprise to Oedipus (f. Bi *recto*).[20] Lydgate avoids this incongruity by supposing that the traveller accidentally lost his way:

> But, for that he failed of a guyde,
> Out of his way he wente fer beside,
> Thorgh a wylde and a waast contre,
> By a mounteyn that stood upon the see,
> Wher that monstres of many dyvers kynde
> Were conversaunt, in story as I fynde. (609–14)

We are never actually told about Oedipus's surprise. Instead, we are allowed to imagine it as we witness the Sphinx's sudden onslaught:

> But of al this Edyppus ignoraunte,
> This dredful hill stondyng on a roche,
> Er he was war gan ful nygh approche,
> More perilous platly than he wende.
> And sodeynly the monster gan descende
> To stoppen his way and letten his passage. (640–5)

The instances discussed above are typical of the concern for logical and effective presentation of the material which pervades the *Siege of Thebes*. They deserve notice, not only because they testify to Lydgate's careful craftsmanship, but also because they suggest that whatever departures from the French we shall henceforth find in the English text are conscious and probably meant to serve a specific design.

The changes which Lydgate makes in the narrative to improve its attitude toward classical antiquity are more subtle but as extensive as those which he makes to rectify its logic. We have already mentioned that Oedipus's decision to travel to Thebes was urged upon him by an oracle. His consultation of the oracle gives the French redactor an opportunity to sneer at what he considers the gullibility of the ancients, whose deplorable ignorance may be inferred from their insistence upon worshipping the sun and the moon instead of the Christian God: 'Or regardez comment les gens estoient adoncques non sachans qui quidoient que le soleil fust dieu et la lune deesse, at laissoient a adorer le createur de toutes choses qui sont sur terre, et adoroient la creature que dieu avoit faicte' (Aiiii *recto*).[21] Lydgate accounts for the entire episode as follows:

> But Edippus wil no lenger dwelle,
> Bu took lieve and in hast gan ryde
> To a temple faste ther besyde
> Of Apollo, in storie as is tolde,
> Whos statue stood in a char of golde
> On wheles four boornyd bright and shene;
> And within a spirit ful unclene,
> Be fraude only and fals colusioun,

Answere gaf to every questioun,
Bringing the puple in ful gret errour,
Such as to hym dyden fals honour
Be rytys used in the olde dawes
Aftere custome of paganysmes lawes.
And Edyppus with ful humble chere
To Appollo maked his preiere,
Besechyng hym on his knees lowe,
Be some signe that he myghte knowe,
Thorgh evidence shortly comprehendyd,
Of what kynrede that he was discendyd.
And whan Edyppus be gret devocioun
Fynysshed hath fully his orysoun,
The fend anon withinnen invisyble,
With a vois dredful and horrible,
Bad hym in hast taken his viage
Toward Thebes, wher his lynage
He heren shal and be certefied. (532–57)

This passage closely resembles its counterpart in the *Roman de Edipus*, where a golden statue of Apollo sits on a four-wheel chariot and Oedipus's question is answered by a 'voix moult horrible' (f. Aiiii *recto*). Lydgate's 'spirit ful unclene' obviously corresponds to the *dyable* who 'habitoit en celuy ymaige qui parloit et donnoit responces a ceulx qui a luy venoient et ladoroient' (f. Aiii *verso*).[22] There is, however, one significant difference between the two documents. Assuming, as we surely must, that the phrase 'be rytys used in the olde dawes/Aftere custome of paganysmes lawes' refers to the term 'honour' in the preceding line rather than to 'errour' in the line before that, the passage may be said to express its author's distrust of the idol but no contempt whatsoever for those who worship it. Since we have posited earlier a progressive change of attitude in Lydgate, we must now note that, just as we find the expression 'non sachans' in the *Roman de Edipus*, so we find the term 'ygnoraunce' contemptuously used in the *Troy Book* to designate the intellectual state of idol worshippers (II, 5533), but there is nothing of the sort in the *Siege of Thebes*.

The attitude of the *Siege of Thebes* toward classical antiquity is again exemplified in the account of Oedipus's marriage. Lydgate is horrified at the perpetration of incest and includes in his text thirty lines of theological considerations which are absent from the *Roman de Edipus*:

> And tofor God is neither feire ne good,
> Nor acceptable blood to touche blood . . . (787–8)

However, he omits a righteous tirade by the French redactor to the effect that the incestuous marriage bears witness to the devil's power over the world in an age when there were only few Christians (f. Bii *recto-verso*).[23]

Most illustrative in this respect is Lydgate's account of Amphiorax, the high priest to whom the Argives turn for advice before undertaking the Theban expedition. The French text presents him as a clever rascal whose ability to predict the future is due to his intimate commerce with the devil (f. Gii *recto*).[24] The English poem, on the contrary, makes him a 'worthy bishop'[25] and an admired and admirable old counsellor whose honest gift of prophecy comes as a reward for his insight into the affairs of the immortals:

> But some [Argives] thoughte ful expedient
> Or they procede to wirke be thavice
> Of on that was ful prudent and right wyce
> And circumspecte in his werkes alle,
> A worthy bisshop into age falle,
> And called was, sothly, by his name
> Amphiorax, of whom the grete fame
> Thorgh all the londe bothen est and south
> Amonges Grekes passingly was kouth;
> A man, in soth, of old antiquyte
> And most acceptid of auctorite,
> First be resoun of his high estat
> And ek for he was so fortunat
> In his werkes, and was also secre
> With the goddys, knowyng her pryvete:
> By graunt of whom, as bookes specifye,
> He hadde a spirit of trewe prophecye
> And cowde aforn ful opynly dyvyne
> Thyngges begonne how they shulde fyne,
> And eke, be craft of calculacioun,
> Yive a dome of every questioun;
> And hadde in magik grete experience,

And fynde cowde be hevenly influence
And by mevyng of the heghe sterrys,
A fynal doome of contek and of werrys. (2794–2818)

We should observe in passing that the discussion of the high priest's achievements progressively narrows from general wisdom to the specific ability to predict the outcome of a war. This organization once again reflects the poet's concern with the effective presentation of his material, for Amphiorax will now proceed to predict the disastrous outcome of the Theban expedition.

Whereas the French redactor assumes the high priest's intrinsic dishonesty, the English poet emphasizes 'his wisdom and his sapience' (2883),[26] and expresses unqualified respect for his prophecies, in regard to which he explicitly denies the use of trickery:

Ful circumspect and riht wel avised,
He hath pronounced in the parlement
Toforn the lordes and the president
His cleer conceyte in verray sikernesse,
Nat entryked with no doublenesse,
Her dysemol daies and her fatal houres,
Her aventurys and her sharpe shoures,
The froward soort and the unhappy stoundys.
The compleyntes of her dedly woundys,
The wooful wrath and the contrariouste
Of felle Mars in his cruelte,
And howe, by mene of his gery mood,
Ther shal be shadde al the worthy blood
Of the Grekes, it may not ben eschewed,
If her purpoos be execute and swed. (2888–2902)

With the next line the narrative shifts to direct discourse, and Amphiorax rises to the level of tragic dignity as he calmly predicts the fate that awaits him before the walls of Thebes:

Depe in the grounds I shal be enclosed
And lokked up in the dirke vale
Of cruel deth. (2908–10)

In one respect Lydgate does much more than merely clean out the belittling remarks of the French text about Amphiorax and lend his character a new dignity. The views concerning war which he attributes to him are in effect those which he himself professes and in support of which he offers the events related in the *Siege of Thebes*:

> Lo! her the fyn of contek and debat.
> Lo! her the myght of Mars the froward sterre.
> Lo! what it is for to gynne a werre.
> How it concludeth, ensample ye may se
> First of Grekys and next of the cyte,
> For owther parte hath matere to compleyne,
> And in her strif ye may se thyngges tweyne:
> The worthy blood of al Grece spilt,
> And Thebes ek, of Amphion first bylt,
> Withoute recur brouht unto ruyne
> And with the soyle made pleyn as a lyne,
> To wyldernesse turnyd and desert,
> And Grekys ek falle into povert
> Both of her men and also of her good;
> For fynaly al the gentyl blood
> Was shad out ther, her woundys wer so wyde,
> To los fynal unto outher syde. (4628–44)

The passage reflects the influence of the epilogue of Chaucer's *Troilus*; but the important thing for us is that the words clearly echo those of Amphiorax himself, so that we need not wonder at the vigour with which Lydgate takes the part of the high priest against the young men who mock his plea for peace:

> This was the clamour and noyse in every cost
> Of hegh and lough thorghout al the hoost
>
> . . . . .
>
> Which of age were but tendre and grene,
> That han not hadde by Martys influence
> Of the werre gret experience. (2933–40)

Lydgate further points to Amphiorax's discomfiture to illustrate his own conviction that wisdom cannot survive without the support of force:

> And wher that foly hath domynacioun,
> Wisdam is putte into subjeccioun,
> Lik as this bysshop, with al his hegh prudence,

For cause he myghte have no audience,
All his wisdam and his profecye
Of the Grekes was holden but folye. (2965–70)

He supports his argument with the truism that even such renowned philosphers as Plato, Socrates, Seneca, Diogenes, Abu-Maaschar, Ptolemy, and Cicero would have spoken in vain if nobody had listened to them. The Argives are, therefore, courting disaster through their refusal to heed Amphiorax's advice, for 'wher prudence can fynde no socour/ . . . Farwel wisdam, farwel discrecioun (3981–4).

When Lydgate sides with the wisdom of age against the recklessness of youth, he puts us in mind of the *Secreta Secretorum* or of Chaucer's implicit approval, in the *Tale of Melibee*, of the 'olde and wise counseillours' (1341) who argue against 'the yonge folk' (1352). But when he goes on to argue for the necessity of a union between force and wisdom, he is also advocating the Renaissance ideal of *sapientia et fortitudo* which we have already noticed in his *Fall of Princes*. Furthermore, when he shows no reservation about allowing his own lesson to be expressed by a pagan priest whom he builds into a symbol of virtue and wisdom, the Benedictine monk John Lydgate expresses a somewhat unmediaeval attitude toward classical antiquity.[27] In the eyes of even those mediaeval philosophers who most respected the authority of Aristotle the wisdom of the ancients was necessarily limited because it lacked the revelation of Christianity. It is significant that Dante made no motion to pull his master Virgil out of hell and that Aristotle himself was not always above the sting of satire.[28] In contrast to this mediaeval suspicion toward the pagan past, Renaissance humanism has been defined as 'the cult of classical antiquity',[29] and we find something of this cult in the later works of Lydgate.

The many didactic passages of the *Siege of Thebes* have not passed unnoticed,[30] but Robert W. Ayers is the only critic to have realized that they are central rather than peripheral to Lydgate's purpose, and to have demonstrated that the message they convey controls the organisation of the entire poem: 'while Lydgate recounts a coherent series of incidents which are related to one another and to the destruction of Thebes, he has employed all episodes to point the central moral message.'[31]

We need not discuss here the details of Ayers's argument, but we may add to his conclusion that the idea of organizing a united tale of heroic adventures around a specific moral concept is likewise the guiding principle of both Spencer's *Faerie Queene* and Milton's *Paradise Lost.*

The *Siege of Thebes* is presented as an illustration of the evils of war, and the solemnity of the intention may be inferred from the high seriousness of the tone in which the subject is introduced:

> I wol reherce a story wonderful
> Towchinge the siege and destruccioun
> Of worthy Thebes, the myghty royal toun. (184–6)

The argument against war is that, regardless of the issue, it grievously injures both the weak and the mighty and crushes vanquished and victor alike; it is the outcome of the sin of pride, and it brings nothing but sorrow to the world (4645, 4653, 4660, 4688). Accordingly, God allows it 'for synne folkis to chastyse' (4659).

If war is both the result and the punishment of sin on a national scale, it can be avoided only if everyone in the nation virtuously performs the part that befits his station in life. The ruler, the nobility, and the commons are bound to each other by specific ties which it is their duty to keep intact. The commons owe obedience and protection to the King, on whose life and authority depends the nation's well-being.[32] The nobility owes the ruler whatever thoughtful and honest advice may be necessary to help him discharge his duty toward the nation.[33] The ruler owes the nation the kind of leadership that will most benefit the entire population, and he can discharge this duty only if he remains unswervingly true to his word.[34] He must especially beware of letting his eminence lure him into despising his subjects:

> And ageyn kynde it is, out of doute,
> That eny hed, be recorde of the wyse,
> Shuld the foot of disdeyn despyse. (262–4)

Indeed, there can be no sovereignty without the love of the nation:

Farwel lordshipe bothe morowe and eve
Specially whan love taketh his leve. (2721–2)

In retrospect we can see that the ideal ruler of the *Siege of Thebes* was not to ascend the English throne until 1558. Writing almost a century and a half before that date, however, Lydgate could do no better than create characters who would not be out of place at the court of Elizabeth. The character in the poem who most nearly approaches the ideal ruler is Adrastus. The *Roman de Edipus* describes him as follows: 'ung roy qui avoit nom Adrascus, moult preudhomme et moult saige, et n'estoit point de la lignee ne de la value des aultres roys qui devant luy regnerent; aincoys fu nay de l'isle de Sicione, filz du roy Chaloy. Et pour le grant sens que Adrascus avoit en sa jeunesse l'eslirent ceulx d'Arges a roy et en firent roy de toute Grece. Celuy roy estoit moult preux et tint bien justice' (f.Cii *recto*).[35] The character of Adrastus in the *Siege of Thebes* is essentially the same as in the French:

. . . Adrastus called was the kyng,
A manly man, riche and wonder sage,
And ronne was somdel into age,
Born of the ile which called is Chysoun,
And whylom sone of the kyng Chaloun;
And for his witt, in story as is kouth,
He chosen was in his tendre youth
Of alle Arge to be crowned kyng
Chief of alle Grece by record of wryting,
Not be dissent nor successioun,
But al only of fre eleccioun
To holde of Arge the sceptre in his hond,
As most worthy of alle Grekes lond,
Loved and drad for wisdom and justice. (1192–1205)

Although Lydgate makes no fundamental changes in the King's character, he makes a very important change in emphasis by stressing qualities which are only mentioned in the French. Thus, the sated compliment 'moult preudhomme et moult saige' yields the much more emphatic 'A manly man, riche and wonder sage'. Within fourteen lines the poet refers thrice to the wisdom of Adrastus and once to his worthiness. In juxtaposition with such expressions as 'manly man' and 'drad', these praises once again illustrate the ideal of *sapientia et fortitudo*. We must note the insistence upon the fact that Adrastus acquired his kingdom by free election rather than by inheritance. On the one hand, it is in keeping with the ideas we have heard Lydgate express about the intrinsic dignity of man and the worthlessness of inherited titles; on the other hand, we cannot forget that the *Siege of Thebes* was probably intended for the perusal of Bolingbroke's son. Some twenty years earlier, in the *Complaint to His Purse*, Chaucer had congratulated Bolingbroke himself on his holding power by free election.

As the action progresses Adrastus lives up to our initial expectations. In particular, he is always careful to preserve with the nobility and the commons the relationship which best serves the cause of the nation as a whole. He never makes an important decision without consulting with the nobility;[36] and his choice of advisers reflects his wisdom as a ruler, for he summons explicitly those 'that wern most manly and most wise' (4117). When he gives his daughters to Polynices and Tydeus, he also gives them half his kingdom, but with the understanding that the two knights will devote themselves to the national welfare (1607–9). In a passage which has no counterpart in the French, Lydgate stresses the King's concern for the little people as he shows him insisting that the humblest soldier be treated with the same diligence as the proudest nobleman (2671–87). Despite his concern with the commons, Adrastus never lays himself open to the same charge as Bolingbroke when Shakespeare's Richard II scornfully accuses him of doffing his bonnet to every oyster wench. What saves Adrastus from the charge of demagogy is the royal quality of magnificence. No matter what the demands of a given situation may be, he always faces them 'ful lik a kyng' (2683) and in 'knyghtly wise' (2571), so that even Eteocles trembles at the mere thought of his 'hegh renoun' (1688). His kindness toward the commons is rather courtesy than flattery, so that he is truly a 'worthy kyng of herte lyberal' (1559). In contrast to the English, the French makes no such attempts at emphasizing the regality of the King of Argos.

The aspect of Adrastus's character most emphasized in the *Siege of Thebes* is his readiness to seek the advice of wise counsellors. We may assume that Lydgate was eager to encourage a similar attitude in Henry V, and it is probably for this reason that the only defect he allows to mar the character of the knight Tydeus is the obstinate unwillingness to heed the advice of men wiser and more experienced than himself. We recall that, when the wise Amphiorax tried to argue against the war, his plea for peace was put down by the younger men, among whom we must necessarily count Tydeus. Later in the poem, Eteocles offers to surrender Thebes with some conditions which Amphiorax advises not to reject without serious consideration. Once again the younger men oppose the High Priest, and it is Tydeus who boldly formulates what they only dare think, for 'he wil have no condiciouns' (3767). The answer which he sends Eteocles has all the superb rashness of youthful valour and none of the caution of age:

> Lat hym not wayte but only after werre.
> The hour is come; we wil it not differre. (3801–2)

The destructiveness of this contempt for advice will be made clear when the war, which Tydeus so enthusiastically seeks, eventually claims his own life. He will not die sword in hand, but ingloriously hit in the back by a bolt from a crossbow as he rides away from battle after a daring sally. Such is the end of unadvised valour; but the victor of Agincourt—if the story was meant for him—did not live to profit by the lesson or even to read it.[37]

Excessive valour is Tydeus's tragic flaw. Otherwise, he is the most perfect knight on earth:

> For every man hath swich opynyoun
> In Tydeus for his gentyllesse,
> For his manhood and his lowlynesse,
> That he was holde the moste famous knyght
> And best byloved in every mannys sight. (2460–4)

The description calls to mind the 'verray, parfit gentil knyght' of the *Canterbury Tales* (*G.P.*, 72); and just as Chaucer writes that his knight 'loved . . . curtesie' (45–46), so the quality which Lydgate's *Siege of Thebes* most emphasizes in Tydeus is that of courtesy. The significance of this observation is that courtesy is perhaps the mediaeval chivalric virtue which the

Renaissance adopted most enthusiastically.[38] Every student of English recalls how Sir Philip Sidney practised it through the very agony of his death on the battlefield.

I have already suggested that Adrastus's behaviour answers the demands of courtesy, and one may occasionally say the same thing of Oedipus.[39] However, Tydeus is the only character in the *Siege of Thebes* in respect of whom we find the concept of courtesy explicitly mentioned. The *Roman de Edipus* introduces him as one 'qui moult estoit preux, hardy, et courtois, et saige' (f. Cii *verso*)[40] and thus emphasizes his courage and boldness. Lydgate does not neglect these qualities, but the organization of his sentence places the emphasis on the courtesy of the dauntless knight:

> Of aventure ther cam a knyght ryding,
> The worthiest in this world lyvyng,
> Curteys, lowly, and ryght vertuous,
> As seith myn autour, called Tidyus,
> Eurous in armes and manly in werkyng. (1263–7)

Tydeus's behaviour immediately justifies each single qualifier in this account. The occasion is his first meeting with Polynices, and the latter's refusal to let him share his shelter has already been mentioned. In the French, Tydeus perceives the futility of the argument and challenges at once the other knight to single combat: 'Thideus . . . bien veit que riens n'y vauldroit soy humilier ne belle parolle, et luy dist que puis que luy convenoit monstrer sa force qu'il se combatroit a luy' (f. Ciii *recto*).[41] In the *Siege of Thebes*, on the contrary, he goes out of his way to appease the insulting Polynices. In the following passage, which again harks back to the *Knight's Tale*, one notices especially the humility and the gentleness which the poet attributes to his hero, as well as the comparison to a knight errant:

> And Tydeus in ful humble wise
> Answerd ageyn of verrey gentillesse
> And seid in soth that of hegh distresse,
> Of the tempest, and the derke nyght,
> He dryven was lich an erraunt knyght,
> Of nede only and of necessite
> And high constreynt of his adversite,

To take loggyng wher so that he myght;
And in that courte therfor he alight
Withoute more, thenkyng non outrage
Nor to no wight noyeng ne damage. (1312–22)

In contrast to the French, the English poem now has Polynices rudely challenge Tydeus, who answers like the ideal aristocrat, taught by good breeding to insist upon receiving his due without ever resorting to improper language. As he vainly appeals to his antagonist's better judgment, he succeeds in uniting the two rare and almost incompatible virtues of firmness and humility:

That is no curtesie
Me to devoyde, but rather vileynye,
Yif ye take hede, that seme a gentil knyght.
And I suppose ye han no title of right
To this loggyng be way of heritage
More than have I, for alle youre felle rage.
And parde yit it shal be no desese
Til tomorowe thogh ye do me ese
Of gentillesse, only with youre leve;
To suffre me it shal litil greve. (1329–38)

His patience, dignity, and courtesy are further impressed upon the reader with the statement that 'ay the more Tydeus spake faire,/Polymyte was froward and contrayre' (1339–40). Tydeus does everything in his power to avoid coming to blows, and he takes up his sword only 'sayng no bettre mene' (1345). Having finally resolved to fight, however, he proves exactly as competent in the practice of arms as he does in the practice of courtesy:

With sharpe swerdes they togyder ryde
Ful yrously, thise myghty championns,
In her fury like tygres or lyouns. (1354–6)

The ideal which Lydgate portrays here is mediaeval, but it is also one which Spenser defines in *Faerie Queene*:

What vertue is so fitting for a knight,
Or for a Ladie, whom a knight should love,
As Curtesie, to beare themselves aright
To all of each degree, as doth behove?
For whether they be placed high above,

Or low beneath, yet ought they well to know
Their good, that none them rightly may reprove
Of rudenesse, for not yeelding what they owe:
Great skill it is such duties to bestow. (VI, ii, 1)

A knight is proved truly courteous only when he succeeds in exercising courtesy under the most trying circumstances. The *Siege of Thebes* places Tydeus precisely in such a position when he goes to Thebes to ask Eteocles to keep his bargain and surrender the throne to Polynices. Tydeus is alone in an enemy city; yet, he boldly enters the castle and seeks out Eteocles, whom he finds surrounded by his vassals. He knows full well that his life is in the greatest danger, but he nevertheless delivers his message with the same graceful courtesy which we would expect in a less precarious situation:

Ful konnyngly he gan the kyng salue,
Requiring hym of kyngly excellence
In goodly wise to yeve hym audience
And not disdeyene, neither in port ne cheer,
Sith he was come as a massagers
From Polymyte, his owne brodere dere. (1894–9)

Because Tydeus is the hero of Lydgate's poem, he must embody the ideal of courtesy. Conversely, because Eteocles is the villain, he must prove the antithesis of that ideal. Accordingly, he turns pale with rage at the mention of his brother's claim, and, after a vain attempt at controlling his temper 'under colour feyned/ . . . To his entent wonderly contrayre' (1958–60), he discards the most fundamental rules of courtesy as he boorishly berates Tydeus for having brought him an unpleasant message:

It scheweth wel that thow were not wis,
But supprised with a manere rage,
To take on the this surquedous massage,
And presume to do so hegh offence,
So boldely to speke in my presence. (2016–20)

By the contrast between the rudeness of Eteocles and the perfect courtesy with which Tydeus has addressed him—'Sir . . . unto your worthynesse' (1901)—Lydgate has emphasized the courtly character of his hero.

The passages examined show Lydgate taking individual details from the *Roman de Edipus* and developing them in a spirit not alien to the English Renaissance. A similar observation may be made about his handling of the narrative as a whole. The French text represents the inglorious end of the favourite mediaeval tradition of romance. It resembles the magnificent *Roman de Thebes* in about the same degree as the comic-book version of *Macbeth* resembles Shakespeare's tragedy, and it is written in the same spirit for an equally naïve audience. If its redactor had any specific purpose beyond that of summarizing into prose a famous and complex metrical romance and availing himself of the fascination which the legend of Oedipus exercised over the Middle Ages,[42] it could not have been one more profound than the listing of exotic adventures in a far-away land. Lydgate, on the contrary, retells the tale with a specific moral purpose: he wishes not only to delight but especially to teach. He raises the tone to high seriousness, as he makes the moral lesson the central organizing element of the poem, to which he thus gives a unity non-existent in the French. The destruction of Thebes is clearly the object of the narrative from beginning to end, and we are never left unaware that it happens through the fault of rulers more interested in their own glory than in the welfare of the nation.

Unlike the French text, the *Siege of Thebes* is a thoroughly nationalistic piece of work. Tydeus, the daring and courteous prince whose death illustrates the futility of unadvised courage, is probably patterned after Henry V, so that the action takes on the emotional immediacy of the conflict between England and France rather than the remoteness of a foreign war of antiquity. Against this background, the prediction of peace which immediately precedes the concluding prayer must be regarded as an encomium of the English rule over western France. In case the reader should fail to perceive the nationalistic intent, Lydgate ends the passage with what has been identified as a quotation from the Treaty of Troyes:

> But love and pees in hertys shal awake,
> And charite, both in length and brede,
> Of newe shal her bryghte beemys sprede
> Throgh grace only in dyvers naciouns,

For to reforme atwixe regyouns
Pees and quyet, concord and unyte. (4698–4703)

The treaty reads, 'Concordia, Pax, et Tranquilitas'.[43]

Considering the high seriousness of tone, the unity of structure, the heroic action, the moral purpose, the concern with the behaviour of rulers, and the national import of the poem, we may allow ourselves a summary statement: if Chaucer's *Troilus and Criseyde* has been called an Italian Renaissance story translated into an English mediaeval romance, then the *Siege of Thebes* might be called a French mediaeval romance translated into an English Renaissance epic. We may also conclude that the attitudes which bring Lydgate nearest to the Renaissance were already present in his work before the second quarter of the fifteenth century.

Chapter Nine

ANOTHER POINT OF VIEW

IN THE PRECEDING CHAPTERS I have taken exception to the practice of considering Lydgate exclusively a Chaucerian and a typically mediaeval poet. I have argued that, although his early works are indeed mediaeval and Chaucerian in nearly all respects, the bulk of his production is only partially so: it is presented in the manner of the Middle Ages and often reveals the influence of Chaucer, but it also expresses certain important attitudes commonly associated with the English Renaissance. The works which have been examined suggest that this dichotomy between content and presentation grew especially noticeable after the completion of the *Troy Book*, although its seeds were already present in earlier poems. To these observations, one should add that Lydgate was the first and only secular poet of his time and country to give such loud and clear voice to the sentiments that were to become literary commonplaces within a few generations. Even Thomas Hoccleve, whose *Regement of Princes* is a precursor of the *Secrees of Old Philisoffres* and an approximate contemporary of the *Troy Book*, devotes so much attention to current events and to his own grievances that he neglects these theoretical aspects of the conduct of rulers which might have appealed to the Renaissance.[1] It is probably for this reason that his work was never printed until the nineteenth century and that its popularity died with its author.[2]

If we accept my arguments, we need not be surprised at Lydgate's popularity with the English Renaissance. We may be more surprised at the approbation, which, as noted in my opening chapter, the Elizabethans expressed about his style. The reasons for that approbation are nowhere explicitly stated, but we may venture to guess that it was prompted by his diction rather than by his fondness for the devices of mediaeval rhetoric. Lydgate is the first English vernacular poet to have made frequent use of the so-called aureate diction, whose rudiments had almost certainly been borrowed by Chaucer from the Latin Middle Ages and Renaissance Italy;[3] and he should probably be credited with having introduced the term 'aureate' into the language.[4]

Aureate diction seeks effect for its own sake and prefers Latinate words to their Anglo-Saxon equivalents. *Macbeth* offers a magnificent instance of it in the sentence, 'No, this my hand will rather/The multitudinous seas incarnadine' (II, ii, 61–62), and we find a more extraavgant example of it in the opening stanza of William Dunbar's *Ane Ballat of Our Lady*:

Hale, sterne superne! Hale, in eterne,
In Godis sicht to schyne!
Lucerne in derne, for to discerne
Be glory and grace devyne;
Hodiern, modern, sempitern,
Angelicall regyne!
Our tern inferne for to dispern,
Helpe rialest rosyne.
Ave Maria, gratia plena!
Haile, fresche flour femynyne!
Yerne us guberne, virgin matern,
Of reuth baith rute and ryne.[5]

The obvious self-consciousness of this diction must have had at least some attraction for the age that eventually accepted stylistic extravagance in the form of Euphuism.

We have seen at the very beginning of the present study that John Metham praised Lydgate especially for his 'halff chongyd Latyne'. The accuracy of Metham's statement has been demonstrated by Isabel Hyde, whose juxtaposition of Lydgate's *Ballade at the Reverence of Our Lady* with the corresponding passage in Alanus de Insulis' *Anticlaudianus* shows that the English poet renders 'oliva fructificans' by 'fructifying olyve' and 'cedrus redolans' by 'redolent cedyr'.[6] In general, the Latinate quality of Lydgate's diction stands out at a glance. In the *Siege of Thebes*, for instance, we see young Oedipus grow momentarily proud as he thinks himself the real son of King Polybus. The aureate quality of the terms used to describe his character is obvious without comparison to a Latin original:

> In herte he was so inly surquydows,
> Malencolik and contrarious,
> Ful of despyt and of hegh disdeyn,
> That no wight durste shortly hym withseyn. (471–4)

At its worst, aureate diction yields pedantic artificiality; at its best, it can lend impressive stateliness to otherwise plain statements. The latter point may be illustrated by contrasting the opening line of Lydgate's version of Venantius Fortunatus's *Vexilla Regis Prodeunt* with an accurate modern translation by Albert Cook. While Cook flatly writes, 'The banners of the King go forth',[7] Lydgate arrests the reader's attention with the majestic statement, 'Royal banerys unrolled of the king'.[8]

The high esteem in which the Englishmen of the Renaissance held Lydgate led them not only to read and praise him, but also to make him a model for their own literary productions. I have already mentioned Farnham's argument that we cannot overestimate the influence of the *Fall of Princes* upon Elizabethan tragedy and his contention that the *Mirroure for Magistrates* was 'conceived merely as an appendage' to that work.[9] We know that the diction of Thomas Sackville's contribution to the *Mirroure* reveals Lydgate's influence,[10] and literary historians have pointed out Lydgatian elements in *Hamlet*[11] and Shakespeare's history plays.[12] Tillyard has shown that Shakespeare drew heavily upon the *Troy Book* for his own *Troilus and Cressida*.[13]

Of particular interest is *The Life and Death of Hector*, printed in 1614 and formerly attributed to Thomas Heywood.[14] Because it is a modernization of *Troy Book* it suggests how the English Renaissance might have handled Lydgate's material. Three of the ways in which the modernized document departs from its original are of importance to us: *The Life and Death of Hector* eliminates some of Lydgate's most abject protestations of inadequacy, occasionally tones down the objections to classical antiquity, and somewhat reorganizes the material.

When Lydgate protests his rhetorical inadequacy, he hardly dares hope that Henry V will condescend to read the wretched stuff with which he presents him:

> I wante connynge, and I fele also
> My penne quake and tremble in my hond,
> List that my lord, dredde on see and lond,
> Whos worthines thorugh the world doth sprede,
> My makyng rude schal beholde and rede,
> Whiche of colour ful nakyd is and bare:
> That but yif he of his grace spare
> For to disdeyne, and list to have pite,
> For fere I tremble that he schuld it se. (II, 144–52)

This is in effect a declaration of intellectual feebleness. The author of the modernization, on the contrary, modifies the syntax so as to suggest only the remotest possibility of stylistic weakness, and he categorically dismisses the very notion that his intended reader may reject the work:

> And kings and princes died by dint of sword,
> Which to recount my hand doth shake for feare,
> Least that my barren wit should not afford
> Fit tearmes and phrases the truth to declare
> Unto my most renowned and soveraigne liege,
> Of all that past in that long ten yeres siege
>
> Which if that he with patience please to heare,
> And not disdaine my rude and simple verse,
> And in his sacred wisedome with it beare,
> While I this wofull historie rehearse:
> Whereof no doubt I have. . . . (pp. 54–55)

When Lydgate asks us to correct his metrical deficiencies he notes that the English language is poor in rhyming words:

> Preying the reder, wher any word myssit,
> Causyng the metre to be halte or lame,
> For to correcte, to save me fro blame:

Late hym nat wayte after coryouste,
Syth that in ryme Ynglisch hath skarsete. (II, 164–8)

However, he takes full responsibility for whatever is wrong with his own rhetoric:

I am so dulle, certeyn, that I ne can
Folwen Guydo, that clerke, that coryous man,
Whiche in Latyn hath be rethorik
Set so his wordis, that I ne can nat be lyke. (II, 169–72)

The modernizer, on the contrary, mentions the lameness of the verse in a conditional clause and lays the entire blame for possible deficiencies on the nature of the English language:

And if my verse for want of skill seeme lame,
Le me intreat you to correct the same.

But blame me not, since the fault's not mine,
For as you know the English tongue is harsh
And wanteth words to make up perfect rime. (p. 55)

We have seen in chapter VII Lydgate turn indignantly upon Homer to denounce him abusively for having condoned Achilles' slaying of Hector and Troilus. We recall the sharpness of his opening injunction: 'O thou, Omer, for shame be now red, /And be Astonyd . . .' (IV, 2784–5). The author of *The Life and Death of Hector* not only softens the tone and tenor of the reprimand, but compensates his cautious disapprobation with a commendation of Homer's eloquence:

But now I must a little change my stile,
And leave the Greeks and Trojans in the fight;
And unto learned Homer speake a while,
Who as it seemes did take a great delight
To praise Achilles for his chivalry,
And all the Greeks t'extoll and magnifie.

But Homer thou has need to blush for shame,
And to condemne thine owne partiality,
For magnifying of Achilles name,
That in thy booke extolst him to the skie:
Who while he liv'd was full of fraud and guile,
And never did deserve so lofty a stile.

I must confesse that with great eloquence,
And rhetoricke, thou hast set forth his praise,
And like a poet of great excellence,
Dost say he was the best knight in his daies.
Yet in one point thou greatly art to blame,
Without just cause to magnifie his name. (pp. 230–1)

This passage is representative of the poem, and the spirit in which it is written comes nearer to the *Fall of Princes* than to the *Troy Book*, though the diffidence with which it presents opinions is quite foreign to Lydgate's poetry.

Considering the two kinds of changes discussed above, we may say that the Renaissance modernizer keeps the material of the *Troy Book*, but attempts either to eliminate or to modify its most typically mediaeval features.

The third kind of change is revealing in another respect. The modernizer occasionally eliminates, abridges, or shifts passages which do not bear directly on the action. His handling of the envoy to Henry V will illustrate the point. In the *Troy Book* the envoy comes naturally after the conclusion of the narrative and ends with two stanzas of 'verba translatoris ad librum suum' (p. 879). The modernizer divides this into three completely separate sections which he presents as if they had no relation to one another, and he prints them before the poem proper as a tripartite 'Epistle Dedicatorie'. He then takes Lydgate's prologue and prints it apart and in italics as 'The Preface'. In so doing, he not only removes from the main body of the poem a section which detracts from its narrative unity, but he also shows an awareness of a fact which has escaped modern critics. Because Lydgate composed imaginative poems with a philosophical intent, he had to explain their meaning to his audience. Because the stories he told were very long, he could not adequately do so with brief introductions or conclusions, as Gower had done for the somewhat shorter tales in the *Confessio Amantis*; like Bernard Shaw, he needed compendious prefaces and appendices. However, he was unfortunate enough to write at a time when there were no provisions for frankly separate introductions and editorial commentary, so that he must necessarily include in his narrative proper much seemingly irrelevant material. The fifteenth century very probably kept the narrative and the commentary clearly distinct. Modern readers, accustomed to the convenience of a critical apparatus, are less likely to make the distinction. With a work like the *Siege of Thebes*, where the commentary governs the organization of the narrative, the failure to distinguish one from the other merely results in occasional impatience at what may be erroneously confused with prolixity; within a work like the *Troy Book*, where the commentary is not structurally related to the narrative, the same failure leads to the uncritical acceptance of Tillyard's rather harsh account of it as 'a shapeless and ingenuous affair'.[15]

Thus, the Englishmen of the Renaissance not only read and praised Lydgate, but seem to have understood him rather better than we do today. Their favourable verdict by no means demonstrates that Lydgate is a better poet than we assume, for each age has its own favourite topics and willingly overlooks the worst deficiencies in an artist who makes these topics his own. Just as modern America will accept almost any author who has Freudian insights and wallows in the hopeless depravity of man, Renaissance England was ready to accept any author who concerned himself with the conduct of rulers and believed in the intrinsic dignity of man. These observations, however, show that there is at least one point of view from which Lydgate may command the respect of sophisticated readers, though we may neither wish nor be able to accept that point of view.

The present practice of evaluating Lydgate by the same standards we apply to Chaucer and the Middle Ages has resulted in both a misunderstanding of his place in the history of English literature and in the unwarranted rejection of his entire production. Trying to evaluate him by the standards we apply to the Renaissance would likewise lead to unwarranted conclusions, since his canons of rhetoric are not those of that period, even though he often expresses its lessons. Nor can we look at Lydgate as the Renaissance did, for we are not the Renaissance, and the sensitivities of a period may not well be transferred to another. We can, however, look at him with the intellectual awareness of what he meant to his own age and to the Renaissance and with the willingness to find what he has to offer, rather than with the determination to find either Chaucer or the limp tail end of the Middle Ages.

Another Point of View

When we look at Lydgate's better works from this point of view, we find a thorough craftsman who occasionally rises to the level of poetic excellence. It will be readily granted that his satire lacks the subtlety of Chaucer's, and his high seriousness reaches in vain for the grandeur of Milton; but his ability to rouse the reader's sympathy is worthy of the greatest names on the roster of poetry. The lesson which he presents is often boldly expressed and, especially in his later works, looks forward as often as it looks backward. These qualities, however, are detectable only if we take Lydgate for what he was: neither a poet of the fourteenth century nor one of the sixteenth, but simply a poet of the fifteenth century in England whose works reflect the intellectual climate of his time and country. In brief, Lydgate can be done justice only if we accept him as a poet in transition.

NOTES

CHAPTER ONE: OPINIONS ABOUT LYDGATE

[1] W. F. Schirmer, *John Lydgate: Ein Kulturbild aus dem 15. Jahrhundert* (Tübingen, 1952), gives 1370 as the date of Lydgate's birth (p. 1) and 1449–50 as that of his death (p. 222). The latter is not agreed upon by all scholars; for instance, A. Brusendorff, *The Chaucer Tradition* (London, 1925), suggests specifically 1449 (p. 214). We know that Lydgate was still alive on October 2, 1446, since he received a royal pension on that date (see J. Zupitza, *Anglia*, III, 532) and he is mentioned as being still alive by Osborn Bokenham, in *The Legend of Saint Elizabeth*, ed. C. Horstmann (Heilbronn, 1883), lines 1075–9, probably composed in 1446 (see introd., p. viii).

[2] The title of 'versifier' rather than that of 'poet' is given to Lydgate by H. S. Bennett, *English Books and Readers 1475–1557* (Cambridge, England, 1952), p. 13.

[3] John Metham, *Amoryus and Cleopes*, in *The Works of John Metham*, ed. H. Craig, EETS, no. 132 (London, 1916), lines 2192–7.

[4] H. S. Bennett, *Six Medieval Men and Women* (Cambridge Univ. Press, 1955), p. 25.

[5] See K. J. Holzknecht, *Literary Patronage in the Middle Ages* (Philadelphia, 1923), pp. 100 ff.

[6] Schirmer, *John Lydgate*, pp. 250–2, lists 178 titles by Lydgate, which he classifies (pp. 229–34) into fifteen categories.

[7] C. Brown and R. H. Robbins, *The Index of Middle English Verse* (New York, 1943), *passim.*

[8] Bennett, *English Books*, pp. 7–8, notes that 'no longer was literature the closed preserve of the ecclesiastic and lord. . . . The growing public evidently absorbed this new-found literature with avidity. . . .'

[9] Bennett, *English Books*, p. 224, writes that 'in the earliest days of printing on the Continent Dr. Haebler has estimated that between four and five hundred copies would be a fair average for a book published between 1480–90. Whether Caxton worked to such a figure we have no means of telling, but it is not unreasonable to think that in a comparatively poor country such as England he did not venture on editions of this size in some of his major works such as *The Golden Legend* or *The Morte Darthur.*' William Blades, *The Biography and Typography of William Caxton* (New York, 1882), p. 142, had suggested editions of fewer than three hundred copies.

[10] Schirmer, *John Lydgate*, p. 223.

[11] We know that an early mediaeval topos required the mention of three names even if the poet intended the praise of only one, as for instance in *Beowulf* ed. F. Klaeber (Boston, 1941), 61: 'Heorogār ond Hrōđgār ond Hālga til.' Although this convention seems to have carried over to the Middle English period, we may reasonably doubt that it was still active during the Renaissance.

[12] John Skelton, *Phyllyp Sparrowe*, in *The Poetical Works of John Skelton*, ed. A. Dyce (Boston, 1856), vol. I, lines 809–10 and 811–19. Skelton also writes that 'It is diffuse to find/The sentence of [Lydgate's] mind' (*ibid.*, 806–7), thus praising the same 'clowdy figures' which are the object of Stephen Hawes's admiration in *The Pastime of Pleasure* (see note 13 below for reference).

[13] Stephen Hawes, *The Pastime of Pleasure*, ed. W. E. Mead, EETS, O.S., no. 173 (London, 1928), lines 22–49.

[14] John Bale, *Scriptorum Illustrium Majoris Brytannie Quam nunc Angliam et Scotiam Vocant: Catalogus* (n.p., 1559), p. 586: 'Joannes Lydgate . . . omnium sui temporis in Anglia poetarum, absit invidia dicto, facile primus floruit. Tantae enim eloquentiae et eruditionis homo iste fuit, ut nunquam satis admirari possim, unde illi in aetate tam rudi, tanta accreverit facundia.'

[15] From a selection in E. Brydges, *Restituta* (London, 1816), IV, 29.

[16] W. Webbe, *A Discourse on English Poetry* (reprinted London, 1871), p. 32.

[17] G. Puttenham, *The Arte of English Poesie* (London, 1589), p. 50.

[18] See, for instance, *Cambridge History of English Literature*, II, 223; and Schirmer, *John Lydgate*, p. 224.

[19] See Schirmer, *John Lydgate*, p. 224.

[20] T. Cibber, *Lives of the Poets* (London, 1754), I, 23.

[21] T. Warton, *Observations on the Faerie Queene of Spenser* (London, 1754), p. 229.

[22] T. Warton, *The History of English Poetry from the Close of the Eleventh to the Commencement of the Seventeenth Century* (London, 1774–81), II, 52.

[23] Isaac D'Israeli, *Amenities of Literature* (London, 1841), I, 314.

[24] Thomas Gray, 'On the Poems of Lydgate', *The Works of Thomas Gray*, ed. Edmund Gosse (London, 1884), I, 397.

[25] T. Percy, 'On the Ancient Metrical Romances', *Reliques of Ancient English Poetry* (London, 1765), III, ix. 36.

[26] S. Turner, *The History of England During the Middle Ages* (London, 1827), V 340.

[27] J. Ritson, ed., *A Collection of English Songs* (London, 1783), I, 1 (i.e. 50).

[28] D'Israeli, *Amenities*, I, 313–14.

[29] T. F. Dibdin, *The Library Companion* (London, 1924), p. 677.

[30] G. Ellis, *Specimens of the Early English Poets* (London, 1801), p. 276.

[31] A. Rey, *Skelton's Satirical Poems in Their Relation to Lydgate's Order of Fools, Cock Lorell's Bote, and Barklay's Ship of Fools* (Bern, 1899), p. 21.

[32] A. W. Pollard, ed., *Fifteenth Century Prose and Verse* (Westminster, 1903), p. xiii.

[33] K. H. Vickers, *Humphrey Duke of Gloucester* (London, 1907), p. 390.

[34] G. Saintsbury, *Historical Manual of English Prosody* (London, 1910), p. 287.

[35] A. K. Moore, *The Secular Lyric in Middle English* (Lexington, 1951), p. 138. Moore, one must add, is by no means so hostile to the entire Lydgate corpus.

[36] E. P. Hammond, ed., 'A Reproof of Lydgate', *MLN*, XXVI (1911), 75, lines 68–77. The poem has been attributed to William de la Pole, Duke of Suffolk, by H. N. MacCracken in 'An English Friend of Charles of Orleans', *PMLA*, XXVI (1911), 142 ff., though the authorship is questioned in Brown and Robbins, *Index*, entry 2178, and is attributed to Richard Roos by Ethel Seaton, *Sir Richard Roos* (London, 1961), p. 126. In assuming the invectives to be directed at the tales of

'Hercules and Dejaneira' and 'Samson and Delilah', in the *Fall of Princes*, I am following Miss Hammond's argument in the preface to her edition.

37 H. Peacham, *The Complete Gentleman* (1625; reprinted Scottish Text Society, 1952), p. 95.

38 E. Cooper, *The Muses Library* (London, 1737), p. 30.

39 R. Thompson, ed., *Chronicles of London Bridge* (London, 1827), p. 239.

40 M. A. Scott, 'Elizabethan Translations from the Italian', *PMLA*, XI (1896), 381.

41 H. S. Bennett, *English Books*, p. 4.

42 Seaton, *Richard Roos*, p. 159.

43 E. Gosse, *Modern English Literature* (London, 1897), p. 35.

44 For instance, F. N. Robinson, 'On Two Manuscripts of Lydgate's Guy of Warwick', *Harvard Studies and Notes in Philology and Literature*, V, 178, prefaces his edition of the text with the statement that 'Lydgate's writings are not of a quality to invite enthusiastic study, but they are of great importance for the investigation of the age just after Chaucer'; likewise, H. Bergen begins his four-volume edition of the *Fall of Princes* (London, 1924–7, EETS, 2nd ser., nos. CXXI–CXXIV) with the argument that, though the poet 'contrives to spoil even his most felicitous passages before he has done with them' (p. xxi), the text is worth editing as 'a document of considerable historical and philological importance' (p. xxii).

45 Schirmer, *John Lydgate*, p. 228.

46 Elizabeth Barrett Browning, *The Book of the Poets*, in *Complete Works*, ed. C. Porter and H. A. Clarke (New York, 1901), VI, 250.

47 T. Lounsbury, *Studies in Chaucer* (New York, 1892), III, 27.

48 H. Bergen, ed., *Lydgate's Troy Book*, 4 vols., EETS, 2nd ser., nos. XCVII, CIII, CVI, CXXVI (London, 1906–35).

49 A. Erdmann and E. Ekwall, eds., *Lydgate's Siege of Thebes*, 2 vols., EETS, 2nd ser., nos. CVIII and CXXV (London, 1911–30).

50 H. N. MacCracken, ed., *The Minor Poems of John Lydgate*, 2 vols., EETS, 2nd ser., no. CVII, and EETS, O.S., no. 192 (London, 1911 and 1934), II, 516–38.

51 See E. R. Curtius, *European Literature and the Latin Middle Ages*, trans. W. R. Trask (New York, 1953), pp. 83–85. Lydgate's use of affected modesty is discussed in chapters IV and VIII of the present study.

52 *A Critical Edition of John Lydgate's Life of Our Lady*, II, 1628–34, J. A. Lauritis, R. A. Klinefelter, and V. F. Gallagher, Duquesne Studies Philological Series II (Pittsburgh and Louvain, 1961). In line 1633 I have substituted 'dewedropes' for the editors' 'dewe, dropes', which seems both arbitrary and confusing; my emendation follows the 1531 print by Robert Redman.

53 Hawes, *Pastime*, lines 1373–4.

54 Moore, *Secular Lyric*, p. 147.

CHAPTER TWO: THE OPINIONS RECONSIDERED

1 Ellis, *Specimens*, I, 273–4.

2 Lounsbury, *Studies*, III, 25–26. The allusion to Mrs. Browning is to *The Book of the Poets*; although she writes that Lydgate 'gives or enforces the occasion for sighing comparison with Chaucer's picturesque vivacity' (p. 250), she pays him some mild compliments as an 'improver of the language' (*ibid.*), 'a voluminous writer of respectable faculties' (*ibid.*), and one who occasionally 'can strike a bold note, but fails to hold it on' (*ibid.*).

3 *Cambridge History*, II, 209–3.

[4] The reference to Samuel Taylor Coleridge is to 'Notes on Troilus and Cressida', in *Literary Remains*, ed. H. N. Coleridge (London, 1836), where Coleridge ranks Lydgate above Gower without giving any specific reason for his preference (II, 130).

[5] G. Sampson, *Concise Cambridge History of English Literature* (1941), p. 85.

[6] E. Legouis and L. Cazamian, *A History of English Literature*, trans. H. D. Irvine (London, 1954), p. 157.

[7] A. C. Baugh, *et al.*, *A Literary History of England* (New York, 1948).

[8] The case for the influence of the audience on the oral-formulaic poet has been clinched by Albert B. Lord, *The Singer of Tales* (Cambridge, 1960), especially pp. 16 ff. See also Lord and B. Bartok, *Serbo-Croatian Folk Songs* (New York, 1951); R. P. Creed, 'The Making of an Anglo Saxon Poem', *ELH*, XXVI (1959), 445; T. F. Mustanoja, 'The Presentation of Ancient Germanic Poetry—Looking for Parallels: a Note on the Presentation of Finnish Runos', *NM*, LX (1959), 1 ff.

[9] *Minor Poems*, I, 329–62.

[10] See L. Conder, *The Church of the Holy Trinity* (London, 1887), p. 49 ff.; also J. B. Trapp, 'Verses by Lydgate at Long Melford', *RES*, N.S., VI (1955), 1 ff. One may wish to argue that Lydgate's reputation as well as the proximity of Bury St. Edmunds were responsible for the selection, but we must not forget that a number of *other* works by Lydgate could have been selected on this basis.

[11] *Crist* III, lines 1495–6, in *The Exeter Book*, ed. G. P. Krapp and E. van K. Dobbie (New York, 1936).

[12] Gray, *Works*, I, 397.

[13] The readings 'Lorde' (272) and 'the' (278) have been substituted for the editors' 'childe' and 'our'. The reading 'lorde' makes better sense and is attested by seventeen manuscripts as well as Redman's print. In view of the statement in line 279, the editors' reading, 'our', seems improbable unless we assume Lydgate to have accused the Virgin Mary of heresy; it is omitted from nineteen manuscripts, and both the Cambridge MS. Kk. 1. 3. and the Redman print have the reading 'the'.

[14] Confessio Amantis, Bk. III, lines 279–86, in *The English Works of John Gower*, ed. G. C. Macaulay, 2 vols., EETS, 2nd ser., nos. LXXXI and LXXXII (London, 1900–1).

[15] Gay, *Works*, I, 399.

[16] All quotations and references to Laurent de Premierfait's *Des Cas des Nobles Hommes et Femmes* and the *De Casibus Virorum Illustrium* are to the excerpts in Bergen's edition of Lydgate's *Fall of Princes*.

[17] P. Ovidius Naso, *Canace Macareo*, in *Heroides*, ed. Henri Bornecque (Paris, 1928).

[18] *Minor Poems*, II, 410–18.

[19] 'The Fickleness of Woman', line 25, in *The Poems of Henry Howard, Earl of Surrey*, ed. F. M. Padelford (Seattle, 1920), pp. 64–65.

[20] *Minor Poems*, II, 382–410.

[21] According to the *OED* the use of this term to denote sexual copulation is recorded in English as early as *c.* 1400, in MS. Bodl. 546, VII, 38: 'The fyxene of the wulf is a sawt ones in þe yeer.'

[22] See in particular *Sir Gawain and the Green Knight*, ed. I. Gollancz, EETS, no. 210 (London, 1940), lines 1460–3.

[23] See Erdmann, *Lydgate's Siege of Thebes*, I, vii.

[24] H. N. MacCracken, 'Studies in the Life and Writings of John Lydgate' (unpbl. Harvard diss., 1907), p. 55; also Erdmann and Ekwall's introduction, *Lydgate's Siege of Thebes*, II, 8–9, implicitly bears out MacCracken's view.

[25] I have discussed this aspect of imagery in Lydgate in 'The Binding Knott: Three Uses of One Image in Lydgate's Poetry', *Neophil.*, 1957, pp. 202 ff.

[26] *Beware of Doublenesse*, lines 48–49, in *Minor Poems*, II, 438–42.

[27] *The Nightingale*, lines 104–5, in *Lydgate's Minor Poems: the Two Nightingale Poems*, ed. O. Glauning, EETS, 2nd ser., no. LXXX (London, 1900), pp. 1–15.

[28] *A Seying of the Nightingale*, lines 358–9, in *Minor Poems*, I, 221–34.

[29] *A Pageant of Knowledge*, lines 160–1, in Minor Poems, II, 724–34.

[30] *Testament*, line 896.

[31] *Ballade at the Reverence of Our Lady*, line 85, in *Minor Poems*, I, 254–60.

[32] *Siege of Thebes*, lines 2296–7.

[33] The *Life of Our Lady*, of which there are forty-three MSS. extant, was printed twice by Caxton about 1484, and once by De Worde in 1531; the *Floure of Curtesy*, of which there is no extant MS., was printed by William Thynne in his 1532 *Chaucer*; and the *Complaint of the Black Knight*, of which there are ten MSS. extant, was printed by Chepman and Myllar in 1508, by Thynne in his *Chaucer*, and by Thomas Speght in his 1602 *Chaucer*.

[34] A. Chalmers, ed., *The Works of the English Poets from Chaucer to Cowper* (London, 1810), pp. 515 ff. and 570 ff.

[35] Ritson, *Bibliographia*, pp. 67 and 70.

[36] See above, chapter I, fn. 28 and text.

[37] Joseph Ritson, ed., *The English Anthology* (London, 1793), I, v.

[38] C. F. E. Spurgeon, *Five Hundred Years of Chaucer Criticism and Allusion* (London, 1914), pp. 15 ff., finds the expression 'my master Chaucer' twelve times in seven works of Lydgate.

[39] See *ibid.*, particularly Henry Scogan (p. 18), Thomas Hoccleve (p. 21), James I of Scotland (p. 34), and Osbern Bokenam (p. 46).

[40] W. J. Courthope, *A History of English Poetry* (London, 1911), I, 325–6.

[41] *Lydgate's Siege of Thebes*, II, 6 ff.; in the temporary preface to vol. I, Erdmann had already suggested the *Roman de Edipus* as the original of the *Siege of Thebes* (p. vi).

[42] See below, ch. VIII, fn. 16, for an account of the scholarship concerned with the sources of the *Siege of Thebes*.

[43] John Lydgate, *The Serpent of Division*, ed. H. N. MacCracken (Oxford and New Haven, 1911), p. 66.

[44] See, for instance, the *Pardoner's Prologue*, line 434; the *Shipman's Tale*, line 101; the *Monk's Prologue and Tale*, lines 1983 and 3458. A slightly different form may be found in other poems, e.g. in the *Manciple's Tale*, line 336: 'hadde ynough suffised'.

[45] Gower, for instance, uses a very similar expression in *Confessio Amantis*, III, 321, and IV, 790.

[46] J. Schick, ed., *Lydgate's Temple of Glas*, EETS, 2nd ser., no. LX (London, 1891), p. 114, in reference to line 1026: 'For unto me it doth inough suffise.'

[47] Sampson, *Concise Cambridge Hist.*, p. 85.

[48] W. Spalding, *History of English Literature* (New York, 1853), p. 86.

CHAPTER THREE: THE PERIOD OF TRANSITION

[1] E. Panofsky, 'Renaissance and the Renascences', *KR*, VI (1944), 208.

[2] J. Nordström, *Moyen Age et Renaissance* (Paris, 1933), p. 13 (my translation).

[3] If any evidence be required to support this statement, R. Guerdan, *Byzantium: Its Triumphs and Its Tragedy*, trans. D. L. B. Harley (New York, 1957), p. 222, has

recently reminded us that the destruction of Byzantium—its people and customs, its monuments, its books—was so complete that its very conqueror, Mohamed II, wept at the sight.

[4] J. Huizinga, *The Waning of the Middle Ages*, trans. F. Hopman (New York, Doubleday Anchor Books A42), p. 323.

[5] See Panofsky, 'Renaissance', pp. 202 ff.

[6] J. Bédier and P. Hazard, *Littérature Française*, rev. P. Martino (Paris, 1948), I, 170.

[7] C. S. Lewis, *English Literature in the Sixteenth Century* (Oxford, 1954), p. 2, particularly in reference to Ludovicus Vives and Julius Caesar Scaliger.

[8] H. E. Hugo, *The Romantic Reader* (New York, 1957), p. 3.

[9] Boileau, *Art Poetique*, in *Oeuvres Poetiques*, ed. L. Coguelin (Paris, n.d.), Canto I, p. 176.

[10] Bédier and Hazard, *Littérature*, I, 170.

[11] See D. W. Reed, *The History of Inflectional N in English Verbs Before 1500* (Berkeley, 1950), p. 284 (*Lindisfarne Gospel*) and p. 285 (five eleventh-century texts).

[12] C. S. Lewis, *The Allegory of Love* (London, 1936), p. 177.

[13] C. Muscatine, *Chaucer and the French Tradition* (Berkeley, 1957), p. 130.

[14] E. M. W. Tillyard, *The English Renaissance: Fact or Fiction* (London, 1952), p. 28.

[15] Lewis, *English Lit.*, p. 25.

[16] *Ibid.*, p. 82.

[17] From *The Poetical Works of Gavin Douglas*, ed. John Small (Edinburgh, 1874), II, 7–8. As I have already suggested, in 'A Note on Virgil's *Aeneid*, X, 229', *N&Q*, CCI (1956), 270, Douglas's translation is faithful enough to help on occasion elucidate obscure passages in Virgil. In view of Douglas's enthusiasm for 'the poet divyne', it is significant that A. C. Brinton, in *Mapheus Vegius and His Thirteenth Book of the Aeneid* (Stanford, 1930), notes that 'the Middle Ages knew Virgil as a man of mystery, a magician; . . . the Renaissance adored him as author of divine allegory . . .' (p. v).

[18] *Vergil's Aeneid*, ed. C. Pharr (Boston, 1930), II, 608–14.

[19] *Aeneis*, II, 824, in *The Poetical Works of John Dryden*, ed. G. R. Noyes (Boston, 1909), p. 547.

[20] C. Day Lewis, *The Aeneid of Virgil* (London, 1952), II, 607–8.

[21] J. W. Mackail, trans., *Virgil's Works* (New York, 1950), p. 38.

[22] J. Seznec, *La Survivance des Dieux Antiques* (London, 1940), p. 7.

[23] *The Gest Hystoriale of the Destruction of Troy*, ed. G. A. Panton and D. Donaldson, 2 vols., EETS, nos. 39 and 56 (London, 1869–74), Vol. I, lines 27–47.

[24] Polydore Vergil, *English History*, ed. H. Ellis (London, 1846), Camden Society, vol. XXXVI, 107.

[25] Joachim Du Bellay, *Les Antiquite's de Rome*, XXVII, 9, in *Oeuvres Poetiques*, ed. H. Chamard (Paris, 1908), I, 25.

[26] *Cambridge History*, III, 209.

[27] Panofsky, '*Renaissance*', pp. 207 and 211 and illustrations no. 7 and 16.

[28] W. F. Schirmer, *Der englische Frühumanismus* (Leipzig, 1931), p. 7.

[29] See *ibid.*, pp. 17 ff.; and E. Walser, *Poggius Florentinus: Leben and Werke* (Berlin, 1914), pp. 71 ff.

[30] See Walser, *Poggius*, p. 87, fn. 3.

[31] R. Weiss, *Humanism in England During the Fifteenth Century* (Oxford, 1941), pp. 19–20.

[32] See M. R. James, *On the Abbey of St. Edmund at Bury* (Cambridge, England, 1895), p. 103.

[33] H. S. Bennett, *Chaucer and the Fifteenth Century* (Oxford, 1947), p. 110.

[34] See J. W. Thompson, *The Mediaeval Library* (Chicago, 1939), pp. 373, 385, 387, 388, 421, and 461.

[35] See Weiss, *Humanism*, p. 25.

[36] See *ibid.*, pp. 30–38.

[37] See *ibid.*, pp. 103–5.

[38] K. H. Vickers, *Humphrey Duke of Gloucester* (London, 1907), p. 342.

[39] See below, ch. IV, footnotes 19, 20 and 21, and corresponding text for a discussion of Lydgate's relation to Poggio's English patron.

[40] See Spurgeon, *Five Hundred Years*, pp. 8 ff.

[41] *Ibid.*, pp. 14 ff.

[42] For the influence of Chaucer, see E. Gattinger, *Die Lyrik Lydgates* (Wiena, 1896), pp. 72 ff. For relationship to the *Gesta Romanorum* and other mediaeval works, see *ibid.*, pp. 13, 38, 50 ff., 60, and 64 ff.; P. E. Sauerstein, *Über Lydgates Aesopübersetzung* (Halle, 1885), p. 6 *passim*; G. Schleich, 'Über der Quelle von Lydgates *The Chorle and the Bird*', *Archiv*, XCIX (1897), 425; J. Duschl, *Das Sprichtwort bei Lydgate* (Weiden, 1912), pp. 48, 55, 86, 88.

[43] For the influence of Chaucer, see in particular W. F. Schirmer, 'Das Ende des Mittelalters in England', *Kleine Schriften* (Tubingen, 1950), p. 25, and T. Naunin, *Der Einfluss der mittelalterliche Rhetorik auf Chaucers Dichtung* (Bonn, 1929), p. 55.

[44] For the sources of Chaucer's *Monk's Tale*, see F. N. Robinson, ed., *The Works of Geoffrey Chaucer* (Boston, 1957), pp. 746 ff.

[45] For the relation of the *Fall of Princes* to Boccaccio, see in particular E. Koeppel, *Laurent de Premierfait und John Lydgates Bearbeitungen von Boccaccios De Casibus virorum illustrium* (Munchen, 1885), and H. Bergen's introduction and notes to his edition of Lydgate's poem, I, ix ff., and IV, 137 ff. For the humanistic aspect of the poem, see Schirmer, 'Ende', p. 33.

[46] For the importance of the ancient classics to the Renaissance see, for example G. Highet, *The Classical Tradition* (Oxford, 1949), p. 15 and *passim*; for the importance of man and the concept of courtesy see Tillyard, *English Renaissance*, pp. 19 ff. and 26ff.; for the rise of nationalism see J. D. Mackie, *The Earlier Tudors* (Oxford, 1952), p. 33.

CHAPTER FOUR: THE MEDIAEVAL TRADITION

[1] W. F. Schirmer, 'The Importance of the Fifteenth Century to the Study of the English Renaissance', *English Studies Today*, ed., C. L. Wrenn and G. Bullough (Oxford, 1951), p. 105, has already suggested a resemblance between the *Complaint of the Black Knight* and the *Book of the Duchess*, though he gives no supporting evidence.

[2] See W. W. Skeat, 'Lydgate's Testimony to *The Romaunt of the Rose*', *Atheneum*, 1896, p. 747, and *The Chaucer Canon* (Oxford, 1900), p. 72; in the latter work, Skeat argues the influence of several other passages in Fragment A.

[3] See J. H. Lange, 'Lydgate and Fragment B des *Romaunt of the Rose*', *Englische Studien*, XXIX (1901), 397.

[4] See L. A. Hibbard, 'Chaucer's Shapen Was My Sherte', *PQ*, I (1922), 222.

[5] As R. K. Root, ed., *The Book of Troilus and Criseyde* (Princeton, 1945), p. 419, points out, Chaucer's line is taken from Petrarch's *Rima*, 182.5: 'Trem' al più caldo, ard' al più freddo cielo.' But Lydgate's wording clearly shows the influence of Chaucer himself.

[6] For instance, B. M. Skeat, *The Lamentatyon of Mary Magdaleyne* (Cambridge, 1897), p. 9, notes the heavily Chaucerian vocabulary; G. Smith, *The Transition Period* (New York, 1900), p. 12, discusses the Chaucerian aspect of the versification, as does E. P. Hammond, 'The Nine-Syllabled Pentameter Line in Some Post-Chaucerian Manuscripts', *MP*, XXIII (1915–16), 129.

[7] See F. W. Bonner, 'The Genesis of the Chaucer Apocrypha', *SP*, XLVIII (1951), 461.

[8] See E. G. Sandras, *Études sur Chaucer* (Paris, 1859), p. 80, and B. ten Brink, *Chaucer Studien* (Münster, 1870), p. 170.

[9] See Schirmer, *John Lydgate*, p. 19.

[10] See P. E. Sauerstein, *Uber Lydgates Aesopübersetzung* (Halle, 1885).

[11] For relationship to the French courtly tradition and the *Romaunt of the Rose*, see Schirmer, *John Lydgate*, p. 26.

[12] For relationship to the *Parliament of Fowls*, see Schick, ed., Lydgate's *Temple of Glas*, p. cxxviii, and G. Stillwell, 'Chaucer's Eagles and Their Choice on February 4', *JEGP*, LIII (1954), 546.

[13] See Schirmer, *John Lydgate*, p. 29. The specific date of the poem is unknown, but Schirmer (*ibid.*) places it definitely in Lydgate's early period.

[14] J. Schnick, *Prologomena zu Lydgate's Temple of Glas* (Berlin, 1889), suggests 1400–2; and again in *Lydgate's Temple of Glas*, p. cxii, *c.* 1403; H. S. Bennett, *Chaucer and the Fifteenth Century* (Oxford, 1948), p. 120, argues for 1410. H. N. MacCracken, 'Additional Light on *The Temple of Glas*', *PMLA*, XXIII (1908), 128, accepts the presence of the Paston family motto in the poem as evidence for taking 1420, the year of Agnes Paston's marriage, as the date of composition. Schirmer, *John Lydgate*, p. 32, accepts this last possibility, but questions the validity of the evidence. However, the presence of a manuscript of the poem in the Paston library, which Schirmer has discussed in 'Ende des Mittelalters', p. 30, adds strong circumstantial evidence to MacCracken's argument. The arguments outlined here, incidentally, make it difficult to accept Ethel Seaton's view that the poem should be removed from the Lydgate canon and attributed to Richard Roos, since Roos was only ten years old in 1420.

[15] See E. Gattinger, *Die Lyrik Lydgates* (Vienna, 1896), p. 35.

[16] Elizabeth Barrett Browning, 'The Book of the Poets', p. 252, considers the poem a precursor of *The Faerie Queen*; I. E. Rathborne, *The Meaning of Spenser's Fairy Land* (New York, 1937), pp. 41–47, and J. W. Bennett, 'Spenser's Muse', *JEGP*, XXXI (1932), 200, discuss the relationship of the poem to Panthea.

[17] For relationship to the *House of Fame*, see Warton, *History*, III, 63, and Lewis, *Allegory*, p. 239.

[18] For relationship to the *Romaunt of the Rose*, see A. Brusendorff, *The Chaucer Tradition* (London, 1925), p. 387; for relationship to Machaut and comparisons with Chrestien, see Lewis, *Allegory*, pp. 239 and 242; for relationship to the *Squire's Tale*, see A. A. Jack, *A Commentary on the Poetry of Chaucer and Spenser* (Glasgow, 1920), p. 108; for implications concerning mediaeval courtly love and the fifteenth century, see H. S. Bennett, *Chaucer and the Fifteenth Century* (Oxford, 1948), p. 120.

[19] The mixture of mediaeval and humanistic elements in the poem has been discussed by F. Brie, 'Mittelalter und Antike bei Lydgate', *Englische Studien*, LXIV (1929–30), 261. See chapter IV for further discussion of *The Temple of Glas*.

[20] In *On the Departing of Thomas Chaucer*, *Minor Poems*, II, 657–9, Lydgate writes that Thomas's absence creates such a 'want' (74) in his life that he is 'pure sory and hevy in . . . hert' (72); see also Schirmer, *John Lydgate*, pp. 51–53, for evidence of the close relationship between the two men and the influence of Thomas's circle upon Lydgate's literary production.

[21] See Schirmer, *John Lydgate*, p. 52.

[22] *Ibid.*, p. 53.

[23] Curtius, *European Literature*, p. 83. The topos of affected modesty is at times merely another form of the so-called humility formula, also described by Curtius, *ibid.*, p. 107.

[24] Pierre de Ronsard, *Lyrics*, ed. S. Savill (London, 1946), p. 68, line 3.

[25] *Ibid.*: 'There will be no servant of yours who, though dozing off on her work, will not suddenly wake up at the sound of my name and bless your own with eternal praise.'

[26] Lines 11–12; this and all subsequent references to Spenser are to *The Poetical Works of Edmund Spenser*, ed. J. C. Smith and E. de Selincourt (Oxford, 1948).

[27] Lines 11–14; this and all subsequent references to Shakespeare are to *The Complete Plays and Poems*, ed. W. A. Neilson and C. J. Hill (Boston, 1942).

[28] *Cliges*, ed. W. Foerster (Halle, 1888), lines 18–21: 'The story which I wish to tell you and repeat is found written in one of the books in the library of my lord Saint Peter in Beauvais.'

[29] *Das Nibelungenlied*, ed. K. Bartsch, rev. H. de Boor (Leipzig, 1949), line 1, 1; the principle here is the same as in the opening lines of *Beowulf*.

[30] See A. Senn and W. Lehman, *Word Index to Wolfram's Parzival* (Madison, 1938), p. 128.

[31] *Minor Poems*, II, 468–85.

[32] *Minor Poems*, II, 486–516.

[33] *The Bruce*, ed. W. W. Skeat, EETS, 2nd ser., nos. XI, XXI, XXIX, LV (London, 1870–89), Bk. I, line 12.

[34] *Minor Poems*, II, 566–99.

[35] Schick, *Temple of Glas*, p. cxii, suggests the date 1398; Schirmer, *John Lydgate*, p. 32, is less specific, but places the poem among Lydgate's very early works.

[36] *Lydgate and Burgh's Secrees of Old Philisoffres*, ed. R. Steele, EETS, 2nd ser., no. LXVI (London, 1894), line 21.

[37] Schick, *Temple of Glas*, p. lvi.

[38] Both Schick, *ibid.*, p. xci, and Schirmer, *John Lydgate*, p. 52, doubt the fact, but recognize the possibility.

[39] The reading *though* (1644) is substituted from Redman's print because the MS. reading *thof* in the quoted edition is confusing.

[40] See Curtius, *European Literature*, p. 160.

[41] See C. F. Babcock, 'A Study of the Metrical Use of the Inflectional *e* in Middle English with Particular Reference to Chaucer and Lydgate', *PMLA*, XXIX (1914), 59; Schick, EETSES, LX, lxiii, likewise notes that Lydgate's language is less indigenous and more modern than Chaucer's; G. Reismüller, *Romanische Lehnwörter bei Lydgate* (Munich, 1911), argues that Lydgate introduces more than eight hundred new Latin and French words into English, besides borrowing about one hundred and fifty already used by Chaucer. J. Miles's study, *Renaissance, Eighteenth-Century, and Modern Language in English Poetry* (Berkeley, 1960), pp. 4, 54, and 58, likewise suggests that Lydgate's poetic vocabulary looks toward the Renaissance.

[42] See, for instance, E. P. Hammond, 'The Nine-Syllabled Pentameter', p. 129.

[43] See F. Pyle, 'The Pedigree of Lydgate's Heroic Lines', *Hermathena*, L (1937), 26.

CHAPTER FIVE: CLASSICAL ANTIQUITY

[1] A good analysis of Hartmann's additions to Chrestien's text as well as of the significance of *mâze* and *triuwe* to the chivalric world may be found in J. Fourquet ed., *Hartmann d'Aue: Erec, Iwein* (Paris, 1944), especially p. 212.

[2] Laurent de Premierfait, *Des Cas des Nobles Hommes et Femmes*, in *Lydgate's Fall of Princes*, IV, 147.

[3] W. Farnham, *The Mediaeval Heritage of Elizabethan Tragedy* (Berkeley, 1936), p. 129.

[4] Guido delle Colonne, *Historia Destructionis Troiae*, in *Lydgate's Troy Book*, IV, 95.

[5] The pagan gods in the *Chanson de Roland*, ed. T. A. Jenkins (Boston, 1924) are considered part of the Mohammedan religion; King Marsilie, for instance, worships Apollo (line 8), and the enchanter Siglorel is taken on a trip through hell by Jupiter (line 1392).

[6] For instance, H. O. Sommer, ed., *The Recuyell of the Historyes of Troye* (London, 1894), I, xl, considers the *Troy Book* the most mediaeval of all Troy stories, and E. M. W. Tillyard, *The English Epic and Its Background* (Oxford, 1954), p. 202, notes that it is extremely mediaeval in spirit. In the context of the present argument, it is interesting that E. K. Chambers, *The Mediaeval Stage* (Oxford, 1903), II, 208, n. 2, considers the poem particularly typical of mediaeval misconceptions about the classical stage.

[7] For the influence of Isidore of Seville and Peter Comestor, see J. D. Cook, 'Euhemerism: a Mediaeval Interpretation of Classical Paganism', *Speculum*, II (1929), 396, and Gilbert Highet, *Classical Tradition*, p. 701, n.

[8] For relationship to Benoit de Sainte More's *Roman de Troie*, which Guido delle Colonne had used for his *Historia*, see D. Kempe, 'A Middle English Tale of Troy,' *Englische Studien*, XXIX (1901), 1, and A. Joly, *Benoit de Sainte-More et le Roman de Troie* (Paris, 1871), I, 494, and II, 895.

[9] For relationship to Jacobus de Cessoli's *De Ludo Scaccorum*, see W. T. Marquart, 'A Source for the Passage on the Origin of Chess in Lydgate's *Troy Book*', MLN, LXIV (1949), 87.

[10] For the influence of Honorius of Autun's *Speculum Ecclesiae*, see H. R. Patch, *The Goddess Fortuna in Mediaeval Literature* (Cambridge, 1927), p. 153; for the influence of Chaucer's *Legend of Good Women*, see C. Brown, 'Lydgate and the *Legend of Good Women*', *Englische Studien*, XLVII (1913–14), 59; for the influence of Chaucer's language, see J. C. Mendenhall, *Aureate Terms* (Lancaster, Pa., 1919), p. 47.

[11] H. Koch, 'Zu Lydgate, *Troy Book*, I, 591: the fyry cat', *Archiv*, CLXXI (1937), 207, discusses Lydgate's borrowing of one expression from Virgil's *Aeneid*; see also E. B. Atwood, 'Some Minor Sources of Lydgate's *Troy Book*', *SP*, XXXV (1938), 25.

[12] For Renaissance elements in *Troy Book*, see Rathborne, *Meaning of Spenser's Fairy Land*, p. 197; Tillyard, *English Renaissance*, p. 32, sees signs of the Renaissance in Lydgate's treatment of women, but, p. 53, he considers the poem generally mediaeval.

[13] A. H. Tilley in *The Cambridge Medieval History* (Cambridge, 1959), VIII, 796.

[14] Curtius, *European Literature*, p. 178, finds the ideal of *sapientia et fortitudo* expressed not only in *The Faerie Queene* and the *Shepheardes Calendar* of Spenser, but also in the works of Boiardo, Ariosto, Rabelais, Cervantes, and numerous other writers of the Renaissance.

[15] Bergen, *Fall of Princes*, I, ix, believes the poem to have been begun in May 1431.

[16] For instance, Gattinger, *Lyrik Lydgates*, pp. 31, 35, 39, 41–42, 65, 70, 72 and *passim*, has demonstrated the influence of the *Legenda Aurea*, Isidore of Seville, and Chaucer on Lydgate's *Testament*, composed about 1445; see also Schirmer, *John Lydgate*, p. 240.

[17] G. Cary, *The Medieval Alexander* (Cambridge, England, 1956), p. 257.

[18] *Ibid.*, Cary notes that 'the theological and moral condemnations of [Alexander] were too firmly established upon the textual evidence, and too obvious to the writer familiar with the most important authorities . . .' to allow a favourable picture.

[19] R. Withington, *English Pageantry* (Cambridge, Mass., 1918), I, 107, argues that Lydgate used classical allegory in dramatic works about one hundred years before any other English author.

[20] *Minor Poems*, II, 695–8.

[21] Since the *Mumming for the Mercers of London* was composed for Mayor Eestfeld, who held the office in 1429 and again in 1437, the work was necessarily composed on one of these two dates; Schirmer, *John Lydgate*, p. 91, favours 1429. The accepted date of the *Mumming at Windsor* is 1429.

[22] Curtius, *European Literature*, pp. 405–6.

CHAPTER SIX: THE PARAGON OF ANIMALS

[1] Tillyard, *English Renaissance*, pp. 19 ff.

[2] G. B. Shaw, *Man and Superman* (London, 1931), p. 103.

[3] I have outlined this principle in greater detail in 'Roland's Lament: Its Meaning and Function in the *Chanson de Roland*', *Speculum*, XXXV, 572 ff., and 'The Heroic Oath in *Beowulf*, the *Chanson de Roland*, and the *Nibelungenlied*', *Studies in Old English Literature in Honor of Arthur G. Brodeur*, ed. S. B. Greenfield (Eugene, 1963), pp. 237 ff.

[4] F. L. Utley, *The Crooked Rib* (Columbus, 1944), p. 31.

[5] F. W. Locke, ed., introduction to Andreas Capellanus, *The Art of Courtly Love* (New York, Ungar, 1959), p. v.

[6] Andreas Capellanus, *The Art of Courtly Love*, trans. and ed. J. J. Parry (New York, 1941), pp. 201–6.

[7] *Bernardus De Cura Rei Familiaris, with Some Early Scottish Prophecies*, ed. J. R. Lumby, EETS, no. 42 (London, 1870), p. 6.

[8] *Ibid.*, p. 7.

[9] For a comprehensive list of similar mediaeval statements about women, see Utley, *Crooked Rib*, particularly introduction, p. 53.

[10] See Lewis, *Allegory*, pp. 2–3.

[11] Ulrich von Lichtenstein, *Frauendienst*, ed. R. Bechstein (Leipzig, 1888).

[12] Machaut relates his own story in the *Voir Dit*. L. Foulet, *Histoire de la Littérature Française*, ed. J. Bédier and P. Hazard (Paris, 1923), I, 88, questions the authenticity of Machaut's account. Even if Machaut invented his own amorous misadventures, however, the very fact that he presented them as real makes the *Dit* representative of the respective positions of men and women at the courts of the fourteenth century.

[13] See Robinson, *Chaucer*, p. 481. Utley, *Crooked Rib*, p. 32, reminds us that Alain Chartier 'aroused a storm of protest' when he expressed rather uncomplimentary views of womankind in his *Belle Dame sans Mercy*.

[14] See Bédier and Hazard, *Histoire*, I, 98.

[15] *Minor Poems*, II, 442–5.

[16] *Minor Poems*, II, 456–60.

[17] *Minor Poems*, II, 438–42.

[18] It is of interest that Lydgate must have written at least one other poem according to the same scheme. His *Ballade per Antiphrasim* (*Minor Poems*, II, 432–3), of which only the first two stanzas and the last two lines are left intact, begins with the statements, 'Undir your hood is but oo contenaunce,/Excludid is from you al doubilnesse,/Unto your herte your tonge hathe accordaunce', and ends with a statement of the satirical nature of the foregoing assertions: 'Thes be as sothe of you, wher that ye be,/As I goo loos, and teied am with a lyne.'

[19] *Minor Poems*, II, 429–32.

[20] *A Ballade of Her That Hath All Virtues, in Minor Poems*, II, 379–81, line 1.

[21] *A Lover's New Year Gift*, in *Minor Poems*, II, 424–7, line 33.

[22] *Black Knight*, lines 498–9.

[23] *Minor Poems*, II, 379–81.

[24] See Lewis, *Allegory*, pp. 2–3.

[25] A. J. Denomy, *The Heresy of Courtly Love* (New York, 1947), p. 27.

[26] Adultery was so frankly accepted as a part of courtly love that Ulrich von Lichtenstein's wife (*Frauendienst*, I, 222, 5 ff.) seems not to have minded in the least her husband's extramarital amorous activities.

[27] *Les Chansons de Guillaume IX Duc d'Aquitaine*, ed. A. Jeanroy (Paris, 1927), p. 1, lines 7–9: 'I have two goodly and gentle mares for my saddle; both are excellent, accustomed to battle, and valiant; but I cannot keep them both, for they cannot stand each other.'

[28] Tillyard, *English Renaissance*, p. 32.

[29] Guillaume de Lorris and Jean de Meun, *Le Roman de la Rose*, ed. E. Langlois (Paris, SATF, 1914–24); the jealous and ridiculously self-conceited husband contemptibly 'chastie sa fame e bat' (8456), particularly in lines 8455–744 and 9361–492.

[30] The Vieille shamelessly whines about the wrinkles which age has substituted for the beauty with which she formerly drove men to despair:

> Mais or m'esteut plaindre e gemir
> Quant mon vis effacié remir,
> E vei que froncir le couvient,
> Quant de ma beauté me souvient,
> Qui ces vallez faisait triper;
> Tant les faisaie defriper
> Que ce n'iert se merveille non. (1264–9)

A little later, she complains about having 'tant . . . ridée la face' (12927) and tells us that her principal consolation consists in remembering 'tout le fait' (12942) of the good old days. One finds many other instances of good women and bad men in mediaeval vernacular literature, as indeed in the literature of any other period, but these instances do not seem to testify to the professional poet's general belief in the equality of the sexes for literary purposes. The two most frequently cited instances deserve notice here. In the *Traité de Morale et d'Economie Domestique* (ed. J. Pichon, Paris, 1846), the Ménagier de Paris's retelling of the stories of Susanna, Lucrece, Criselda (I, 64–68; 70–75; 99–125), and others, and his regret that husbands often cause that 'les bonnes dames . . . eient tant à souffrir' (I, 124–5) are matched by the story of Raymonds (I, 68–70) and the assertion that God rightfully cursed Eve and her daughters for the sin whose consequences we must bear to this day: 'par inobédience et orgueil grant mal et mauvaise conclusion vient . . . comme on lit en la Bible de Eve, par la désobéissance et orgueil de laquelle elle et toutes celles qui aprè elle sont venues et vendront, furent et ont esté par la bouche de Dieu mauldictes' (I, 128). And then, a domestic treatise by a Parisian burgher can hardly be considered typical of the views of mediaeval court poets, even if it was written with the encouragement of Charles V, who also encouraged the shepherd Jean de Brie to produce a treatise on his art. *Le Livre du Chevalier de La Tour Landry* (ed. A. de Montaiglon, Paris, 1854) is harder to dismiss because its author was a knight and its great popularity extended beyond France to Germany and England. Here the good knight voices his horror at the multitude of men who betray women 'sanz cause et sanz raison' (p. 3), without either 'paour ne honte' (*ibid.*), and he presents his book as a record of 'les bonnes meurs des bonnes dames et leurs biens faiz' (*ibid.*). Despite this pro-feminine statement of purpose, however, the *Livre* contains fairly few specific instances of male misbehaviour and female worthiness, while it fills page after page with anecdotes illustrating practically every sin a woman can possibly perform. Although we can only hope that it had its intended result of encouraging the author's daughters to turn 'à bien et à honneur' (*ibid.*, p. 2), the male reader with a concern for his own welfare will surely be discouraged from further intercourse with women. It is of interest that the Middle-English translation, *The Book of the Knight of La Tour-Landry* (ed. T. Wright, EETS, o.s., XXXIII, London, 1906), is somewhat more violent than the French. When the French, for example, shows 'la femme du roy Pharaon' (p. 120) attempting to seduce Joseph, we are told that she 'lui monstra moult de folz signes d'amours par regars et par autres folz semblans . . .' (p. 121); to the woman's erotic folly described here, the English must explicitly attach the label of sin: 'she shewed hym mani foly signes and semblauntz of fals love and sinfull' (p. 76).

31 E. T. Donaldson, 'Chaucer the Pilgrim', *PMLA*, LXIX, 936.

32 B. H. Bronson, *In Search of Chaucer* (Toronto, 1960), p. 66.

33 Utley, *Crooked Rib*, p. 26.

34 For a list of Lydgate's female patrons, see Holzknecht, *Literary Patronage*, pp. 100–1.

35 Utley, *Crooked Rib*, p. 64.

36 See *ibid.*, p. 71.

37 Utley, *ibid.*, p. 69, reminds us that 'when we speak of the feminism which begins with the Renaissance it is largely of such educators as Vives that we are thinking'.

38 *Ibid.*, pp. 84–85.

39 Farnham, *Medieval Heritage*, p. 293.

40 *Minor Poems*, II, 574–8; see below, VII, note 19 and text for Lydgate's extension of this view to the nature of regality.

41 In the *Romant de la Rose*, Nature presents a similar argument from a negative point of view, thus suggesting that a nobleman by birth may in reality be no nobleman at all, but not that anyone may become a nobleman by acting like one:

> Souz cet fais deit cil toujourz vivre
> Qui gentis on veaut resembler,
> S'il ne veaut gentillece embler
> E senz deserte los aveir.
>
> . . . . .
>
> . . . nus ne deit eveir loenge
> Par vertu de persone estrange. (18798–808)

As Robinson points out in the notes, the argument to which the quotation from the

Wife of Bath's Tale is a conclusion comes from Dante's discussion of the nature of nobility, in the *Convivio*.

42 The present argument does not reflect a change from the view expressed in ch. IV above, and in 'Attitudes Toward Women in Lydgate's *Siege of Thebes*', *ES*, XLII, 1 ff., that the *Temple of Glas* is in other respects a very conventional poem. Indeed, it is significant that the first unhappy woman in the poem is Dido herself.

CHAPTER SEVEN: THE NATION AND THE PRINCE

1 'A Worcester Fragment', ed. B. Dickins and R. M. Wilson, *Early Middle English Texts* (New York, 1951), p. 2, lines 9–17. William the Conqueror's concern with the possibility of native uprisings suggests that nationalism was a force among the English immediately after the Conquest. See A. L. Poole, *From Domesday Book to Magna Charta* (Oxford, 1955), p. 102.

2 See 'The Languages of England', *The Chronicle of Robert of Gloucester*, in *Early Middle English Texts*, p. 14.

3 See 'The Author and His Sources', *Laȝamon's Brut*, *ibid.*, p. 20.

4 For instance in the *Bruce*, ed. W. M. MacKenzie (London, 1909), the Scots Barbour reproaches John Balliol with having 'stuffyt all [Scotland] with Inglis men/ . . . sa ryht fellone,/And sa wykkyt and covatous,/And swa hawtane and dispitous,/That Scottis men mycht do na thing/That evir mycht pleys to thar liking' (I, 189–98), and he likens his own compatriots 'to the Machabeys,/That, as men in the Bibill seys,/Throw thair gret worschip and valour,/Fawcht in-to mony stalwart stour,/For to delyvir thar countre/Fra folk that, throw iniquite,/ Held thaim and thairis in thrillage' (I, 465–71). The English Minot, on the other hand, assures us (*The Poems of Laurence Minot*, ed. J. Hall [Oxford, 1897]) that all Scots 'er ful of gile' (II, 6), while King Edward is fighting 'in his right' (I, 31), and that 'oure Inglis men' (e.g. IV, 44; V, 72) are so gallant that the French who 'fals treson alway . . . wroght/ . . . fro thai met with Inglis men,/All thaire bargan dere thai boght' (VII, 62–64). These examples, however, are not necessarily indicative of a pervasive national spirit like that of Victorian England, since they reflect principally Barbour's legitimate exasperation with the invader and Minot's contempt for the enemy, especially when he is defeated.

5 S. Painter, *A History of the Middle Ages* (New York, 1953), p. 365.

6 Alain Chartier, *Le Quadrilogue Invectif*, ed. R. Bouvier (Paris, 1944), especially pp. 75 ff.

7 See Painter, *History*, p. 366.

8 *Minor Poems* II, 710–22.

9 G. B. Shaw, *Saint Joan* (London, 1932), p. 97.

10 *Troy Book* ends, in fact, on a deeply patriotic note; but since the passage in question is primarily an encomium of Henry V for the benefit of Henry V, the evidence it brings to bear on Lydgate's patriotism must not be accepted [totally] uncritically.

11 The passages quoted from Boccaccio and Laurent are printed in the notes to *Lydgate's Fall of Princes*, IV, 396.

12 *Minor Poems*, II, 539–66.

12[a] F. L. Utley, ed., *The Forward Movement of the Fourteenth Century* (Columbus, 1961), p. 3.

13 In this respect it is significant that the term 'nationalism' does not rate a single entry in the index to *The Cambridge Medieval History*, while it is listed three times (for pp. 88, 88–89, 194) in the first volume of *The New Cambridge Modern*

History (Cambridge, 1957) for the years 1493–1520; in the latter volume, R. Aubenas speaks of the new 'rebellious nationalist feeling' (p. 86), and R. G. D. Laffan mentions the 'rising consciousness of . . . nationality' (p. 194). It may likewise be of some significance that the term 'patriot' in its modern sense is not recorded in the *OED* until 1605.

14 See above, notes 1, 2, 3, 4.

15 For instance, Lydgate advises rulers to be kind to strangers, so as to avoid being killed like King Lamedon (II, 82 ff.); he advises them to think twice before starting a war, lest they be killed like King Priam (II, 1889 ff.); and he advises Henry V to devotion, so that God may grant him a long reign (V, 3581 ff.). In none of these instances does he specifically consider the ruler's relation to the nation or advise him to live up to any ideal other than that of personal success.

16 L. T. Smith, *Gorboduc* (Heilbronn, 1883), p. xxi, has argued in favour of 1400 on the basis of a statement in the manuscript, and Schick, *Temple of Glas*, p. cxii, accepts that date. However, MacCracken, in his edition of the *Serpent of Division* (London, 1911), p. 4, and in 'Lydgate's *Serpent of Division*', *MLR*, VIII (1913), 103, presents far more convincing arguments in favour of 1422.

17 *Minor Poems*, II, 624–30, lines 41–45, 56, 123–4, 126, 134.

18 Laurent wrote two versions of the work; *Des Cas des Nobles Hommes st Femmes* is the title normally used today for the second version as printed in Paris by Jean du Pré in 1483 as *Des Cas et Ruyne*, and again in Paris by Antoine Vérard in 1494 and 1506 [?], by Nichel Le Noir in 1515, and by Nicholas Couteau in 1538 as *Des Nobles Maleureux*; the first version was printed as *De la Ruyne* in Bruges by Colard Mansion in 1476, and in Lyons by Huss and Shabeler in 1483.

19 See, for instance, I, 260 ff.; IV, 1146 ff.; VI, 1282 ff. The same idea, borrowed with due acknowledgment from Dante's *Convivio*, is found in Chaucer's *Wife of Bath's Tale*, line 1109 ff. See above, VI, note 40 and text, for argument that Chaucer, however, puts the argument in the mouth of a grotesque old hag ludicrously trying to convince a handsome knight to make love to her; furthermore, Chaucer himself is thrice removed from the opinion expressed, since it is spoken by a literary character in a story narrated by another literary character. Lydgate, on the other hand, expresses the opinion in all seriousness and assumes full responsibility for it.

20 John of Salisbury, *Policraticus*, ed. C. C. J. Webb (Oxford, 1911), has such contempt for the illegitimate 'tyrant', in contradistinction to the legitimate 'prince', that he writes 'tyrannum occidere non modo licitum est sed aequum et iustum' (I, 232 [bk. III, 15]), but he further explains that the principal difference between the two is that the legitimate prince respects the law while the tyrant does not. Lydgate's immediate predecessor, John Gower, had expressed with greater caution somewhat similar views in the *Vox Clamantis*, ed. G. C. Macaulay, *The Complete Works of John Gower* (Oxford, 1902), VI, 1–314, especially bk. VI, viii, 605–10; but like John of Salisbury he had written in Latin so that his lesson, unlike Lydgate's, was addressed to a relatively restricted audience of learned men.

21 For instance, we find the opinion in Henry Medwall's *Fulgens and Lucres*, ed. F. S. Boas and A. W. Reed (Oxford, 1926): 'I do hym commend/As the more noble man sith he . . ./By mean of hys vertue to honoure doth aryse' (II, 752–4). It is more specifically expressed in Medwall's source, John Tiptoft's *Declamacion of Noblesse*, printed by Caxton in 1481, where we learn that in a certain respect the poorest man may be the equal of a king (ff. f. 3*verso*-4*verso*). The *Declamacion* is itself a translation, probably through Mielot's French text, of Buonaccorso de Montemagno's *Controversia de Nobilitate*, written about two years before Lydgate began the *Fall of Princes*.

[22] John of Salisbury, *Policraticus*, I, 236, writes that, though the legitimate ruler may prove unsatisfactory, he who opposes him 'Dei ordinationi resistit' (bk. IV, 1).

[23] In *Lydgate's Fall of Princes*, IV, p. 261: 'with God's tolerance, they have become rulers in the world through manslaughter, theft of countries, and a thousand other acts of violence'.

[24] For examples of the inhumanity of the many poor men who rose to power during the fifteenth century, see Huizinga, *Waning of the Middle Ages*, pp. 28 ff.

[25] According to the line numbering in Steele's edition, Lydgate wrote 1491 lines of the *Secrees*; the remainder is by his disciple, Benedict Burgh.

[26] Line 2367 ff. in Burgh's continuation.

[27] See DeWitt T. Starnes's introduction to John Lydgate, *The Governaunce of Kynges and Prynces* (Gainesville, 1957), pp. v ff.

[28] Farnham, *Medieval Heritage*, p. 277.

[29] *Ibid.*, p. 61.

CHAPTER EIGHT: THE STORY OF THEBES

[1] I have already mentioned Lydgate's own testimony that he began the *Troy Book* in 1412; and Bergen, *Fall of Princes*, I, x, argues that the *Fall of Princes* was finished in 1438–9. Between these two dates Lydgate must have devoted the major part of eight years to the *Troy Book*, one year to the *Siege of Thebes*, and another eight years to the *Fall of Princes*: a total of at least seventeen years.

[2] E. Koeppel, *Lydgate's Story of Thebes* (Munich, 1884), pp. 11 ff., argues that the poem was begun in 1421 and finished in 1422. In their notes to *Lydgate's Siege of Thebes*, A. Erdmann and E. Ekwall, eds., argue that 'the greater part of the poem was written in the course of 1421' (II, 10); and J. Parr, 'Astronomical Dating for Some of Lydgate's Poems', *PMLA*, LXVII (1952), 256, demonstrates that the prologue must have been composed in 1421.

[3] See G. A. Panton and D. Donaldson, eds., *The Gest Hystoriale of the Destruction of Troy*, EETS, no. 39 (London, 1874), p. xlix.

[4] At least, Lydgate feels compelled to refer to the *Monk's Tale* at the beginning and at the end of the *Fall of Princes* (I, 349; IX, 3427).

[5] See my 'Chaucerian Character Names in Lydgate's *Siege of Thebes*', *MLN*, LXXI (1956), 249 ff.

[6] The relationship between the *Siege of Thebes* and the *Canterbury Tales* has been a fruitful field of investigation. See in particular B. ten Brink, *English Literature*, trans. Kennedy (London and New York, 1887–92), II, pt. 1, p. 225; E. P. Hammond, *Chaucer: a Bibliographical Manual* (New York, 1933), p. 317, and 'Lydgate's Prologue to the Story of Thebes', *Anglia* (1912), XXXVI, 360 ff.; Lewis, *Allegory*, p. 162 and *passim*; and the notes to Erdmann and Ekwall's edition.

[7] See L. Constans, *La Légende d'Oedipe* (Paris, 1881), pp. 156 ff. I have discussed the problem in 'Thebes, Troy, Criseyde, and Pandarus: an Instance of Chaucerian Irony', *SN* (1960), XXXII, 14.

[8] H. N. MacCracken, 'Studies', pp. 54 f.

[9] Lydgate mentions 'Stace of Thebes' in line 1272. For advice to royalty, see Publius Popinius Statius, *Thebaid*, ed. T. Ethelbert (London, 1928), I, 406–645, and X, 176–218. When the Greek host arrives within sight of Thebes, King Eteocles seeks advice from Tiresias and is submitted to a lengthy discourse; later, when the conquest of Thebes proves a more serious undertaking than the Argives had anticipated, King Adrastus calls his chieftains to a council about the conduct of the war and is advised by them.

If, as A. Joly has suggested in *Benoit de Sainte-More et le Roman de Troie* (Paris, 1871), I, 494, and II, 895, Lydgate drew on the *Roman de Troie* while composing the *Troy Book*, he was probably acquainted with the *Roman de Thebes*, since that work is almost always bound in the same MSS. with the *Roman de Troie*. It is therefore significant that the *Roman de Thebes*, ed. L. Constans (Paris, 1890), also contains instances of advice to kings, particularly in lines 1115–52, 2053–70, 3497–662, 4951–5128, and 8196–406. Lydgate occasionally refers to his 'auctour' (e.g. line 199), but he never names either him or his work.

10 *Siege of Thebes*, II, 2.

11 *Siege of Thebes*, lines 177–89, 324, 1044–6, 1047–59, 4520–4, and 4604–7. For a larger count, see Erdmann and Ekwall's notes to their edition, II, 2–3; some of the references which they point out have been discounted here because they are not clear enough to serve as unquestionable evidence.

12 Bennett, *Chaucer*, p. 139, argues that Lydgate's scheme was his way of paying his literary debt to Chaucer. On the other hand, W. H. Schofield, *English Literature from the Norman Conquest to Chaucer* (New York, 1906), sees only 'bad judgment and presumption' (p. 297) in Lydgate's attempt to connect his poem with the *Canterbury Tales*.

13 Curtius, *European Literature*, pp. 83 and 85.

14 *Siege of Thebes*, line 183; discussed in chapter I.

15 Curtius, *European Literature*, p. 184.

16 E. Koeppel, *Lydgate's Story of Thebes* (Munich, 1884), p. 52, was the first scholar to argue that the English poem was based on a prose redaction of the *Roman de Thebes*, and he suggested the *Ystoire de Thebes*. As illustrated by Constans (*Légende*, pp. 366–7), the common assumption until then was that Lydgate had followed either the *Roman de Thebes* itself or a fictitious imitation of it allegedly written in Latin by Chaucer. Since then, Erdmann has demonstrated in the notes to his edition (II, 6–7) that Koeppel's theory was correct but that Lydgate's original must have been the *Roman de Edipus* rather than the *Ystoire de Thebes*. The only weakness of his argument is that many character names and four passages in the *Siege of Thebes* seem nearer to the *Ystoire de Thebes* than to the *Roman de Edipus*. In 'Chaucerian Character Names in Lydgate's *Siege of Thebes*', I have shown that the negative evidence of the character names may be disregarded; and in 'The Immediate Source of Lydgate's *Siege of Thebes*', *SN*, XXXIII, 86 ff., I have argued that we may consider the *Roman de Edipus* the original of the *Siege of Thebes*. There is only one extant MS. of the romance (*MS. 3C1*, fonds francais, at the French National Library) and one early sixteenth-century printing by Pierre Sergent (*Le Roman de Edipus, Filz du Roy Layus, Lequel Edipus Tua Son Pere. Et Depuis Espousa Sa Mere et en Eut Quatre Enfants: Et Parle de Plusieures Choses Excellentes*). All my references and quotations are from the facsimile print of Sergent's text (Paris, 1858).

Since, as I have pointed out in 'A Note on the Prose Redaction of the *Roman de Thebes*', *N & Q*, CC (1955), p. 508, the exact relationship between the *Roman de Edipus* and the *Ystoire de Thebes* has not yet been established beyond question, it is not utterly impossible that the MSS. of the *Roman de Edipus* used by Lydgate presented some features now extant only in the *Ystoire de Thebes*. Whenever relevant to the argument, my notes indicate the rare occasions when Lydgate's departures from the *Roman de Edipus* might be explained by assuming his familiarity with the text of the *Ystoire de Thebes*. References to the latter text are to the print by Antoine Vérard, in *Les Histoires de Paul Orose Traduites en François* (Paris, 1491).

17 If Lydgate were following the French text, the name of Oedipus would probably appear in line 437. The inconsistency does not exist in the *Ystoire de Thebes*; however, the statement in that document that Oedipus was so named

because his feet were tied together—'il avoit les piedz liez' (f. Lxxiii *recto*)—differs from the explanation in both the *Roman de Edipus* and the *Siege of Thebes*, so that we may assume the improvement to be Lydgate's own work.

18 Jocasta tells her story in lines 912–41; the executioners are last seen going 'toward Thebes' in line 432.

19 'Ceste beste avoit la contree si effrayee par la cruaulte . . . que il ny osoit aller ne venir nulle creature.'

20 'Edipus . . . percrue ce ne fut mye merveilleuse chose sil en eut grant doutance.' The *Ystoire de Thebes* is even more emphatic on this point: 'il fut moult esbahy et ne scavoit que faire' (f. Lxxi *verso*).

21 'See, therefore, how ignorant the people were in those days, since they believed the sun to be god and the moon goddess, and they failed to adore the creator of all things that are on earth, and they adored the creation which God had made.' The *Ystoire de Thebes*, f. Lxxi *recto*, goes farther, and even seizes upon the occasion to remind the reader how much better things are since the New Testament.

22 '[The devil who] lived within this statue and spoke and gave answers to those who came to him and worshipped him.'

23 I interpret the phrase 'gens quit creussent en dieu' to mean 'Christians'.

24 In this respect the *Ystoire de Thebes*, f. iiiiXXv *verso*, is even more specific than the *Roman de Edipus*. It is interesting that the *Roman de Thebes*, ed. Léopold Constans (Paris, 1881), lines 5105 ff., is much more respectful of the high priest than either of the prose redactions.

25 Lydgate may have taken his cue from Chaucer's *Troilus and Criseyde*, II, 104–05: 'the bisshop . . ./Amphiorax'.

26 It is true that when Amphiorax is finally swallowed by the earth and received in hell, Lydgate points to his fate as the just reward of idolatry. However, the significance of the passage in respect to Lydgate's attitude is highly questionable on at least two counts: (1) the passage expresses an attitude unparalleled anywhere else in the poem and in direct contradiction to the prevalent attitude, and (2) it is almost surely an attempt at reminding us of the conclusion of Chaucer's *Troilus and Criseyde*, for the similarity in wording is too great to be accidental: 'Lo! here the mede of ydolatrie . . . ,/Lo! what avayllen incantaciouns' (4047–9).

27 J. C. McGalliard, 'Classical Mythology in Certain Treatments of the Legends of Troy, Thebes, and Aeneas: a Study in the Literary Paganism of the Middle Ages' (Harvard upubl. diss., 1930), p. 216, has argued in regard to French romances that mediaeval authors knew that the Greeks and Romans were pagans, but they did not comprehend the meaning of paganism and would occasionally imagine them as Christians. We might be tempted to formulate a similar argument about the treatment of Amphiorax in the *Siege of Thebes*, but the testimony of the *Troy Book* has made it clear that, however badly Lydgate may have understood the pagans, he did not think of them as Christians.

28 For instance, in the *Lai d'Aristote*, ed. L. d'Aussy, *Fabliaux ou Contes* (Paris, 1829), pp. 373 ff., the thirteenth-century *trouvère* Henri d'Andeli has the aged Aristotle make an utter fool of himself by getting down on all fours to allow a young woman to bridle and saddle him and ride on his back. The yarn is obviously connected to the Alexander exempla, and seems intended to show that philosophers in general, rather than Aristotle in particular, are incapable of acting according to their own precepts. Yet it is significant that Henri selected a pagan philosopher rather than a Christian to illustrate the point. The attitude suggested here is likewise detectable in his *Bataille des VII Arts*, ed. J. Paetow (Berkeley, 1914), where the pagans' behaviour is even more ridiculous (e.g. lines 186 ff.) than that of their Christian followers.

29 E. Underhill, *Cambridge Medieval History*, VII, 769.

30 See, for instance, Erdmann and Ekwall's notes to their edition of the poem, II, 14; and Schirmer, *John Lydgate*, p. 56.

31 R. W. Ayers, 'Medieval History, Moral Purpose, and the Structure of Lydgate's *Siege of Thebes*', *PMLA*, LXXII (1958), 471.

32 For instance, when Creon ascends the throne of Thebes, his subjects swear 'to be trewe . . ./To hym only with body and with good' (4393–4); after Laius's death, the Thebans are shown in dire straits for lack of 'a governor,/Ayeynst her foon havyng no socour/hem to defence' (757–9); and the death of Eteocles brings momentary confusion because 'though so be comownerys be stronge/With multitude and have no governaylle/Of an hed, ful lytyl may avaylle' (4380–2).

33 For instance, after Laius's death, the 'lordes all' of Thebes advise Jocasta to remarry for the good of the city (763–77), and they are later classified according to the honesty of the advice they give Eteocles (1715–20).

34 For instance, we are told that the ruler must put his people's welfare before his own, because 'in a prince it is ful gret offence/ . . . Yif he habound and [his people] han right noght' (2688–92), and that the destruction of Thebes came about simply because Eteocles's 'biheestes trewly wern not holde' (2548).

35 'A king who was named Adrastus, very brave and wise, and who was not of the lineage and rank of the other kings who reigned before him; rather, he was born on the Island of Sicione [and was] King Chaloy's son. And because of his sound judgment, the people of Argos elected him king in his youth and made him king over all Greece. This king was very brave and rendered justice adequately.'

36 See, for instance, *Siege of Thebes*, 2573, 2788–93, and 4107–12, where Adrastus calls for advice regarding the decision to declare war on Thebes, the conduct of the hostilities, and the appointment of a high priest.

37 See Erdmann and Ekwall, *Siege of Thebes*, introduction, II, 8–9.

38 See Tillyard, *English Renaissance*, pp. 32–34. R. J. Mitchell, 'Italian "Nobilità" and the English Idea of the Gentleman in the XV Century', *EM*, IX (1958), has demonstrated that the English concern for 'the rules of knightly conduct and behaviour' (p. 23) came principally from Italy and developed during the second half of the fifteenth century.

39 Oedipus's decision to leave Arcadia and go to Thebes will illustrate the point. In the *Roman de Edipus* (f. Aiii *recto-verso*) he breaks in on King Polybus to demand an explanation about his own status and rudely announces his plan to go away; in the *Siege of Thebes*, on the contrary, he politely waits for 'opportune space' (503) to kneel before the King and formulate his request according to the rules of courtesy.

40 '[One] who was very brave, bold, and courteous, and wise.'

41 'Thideus . . . clearly saw that he would gain nothing through self-humiliation or kind words, and told him that since he must use force he would fight him.'

42 See Constans, *Légende d'Oedipe*, pp. 95–141, according to whom the legend of Oedipus was not only familiar enough to the learned to be treated in Mediaeval Latin poetry, but popular enough to become the source of a great many tales of incest between mother and son, e.g. the legend of Judas in the *Legenda Aurea*, the legend of Saint Gregory (whose most important treatments are the *Vie du Pape Gregoire*, the *De Mirabili Divina Dispentione et Ortu Beati Gregori Pape* in the *Gesta Romanorum*, and Hartmann von Aue's *Gregorius*), the *Vita Sancti Albini*, the *De Amore Inordinato* in the *Gesta Romanorum*, and the *Dit du Buef*.

43 *Tractatus Trecensis*, item 24, ed. T. Rymer, *Foedera* (The Hague, 1740), III, 173. For identification with Lydgate's text, see Erdmann and Ekwall, *Siege of Thebes*, II, 8–9 and 136.

CHAPTER NINE: ANOTHER POINT OF VIEW

1 Thomas Hoccleve, *Regement of Princes*, in *Works*, ed. F. J. Furnivall, EETS, 2nd ser., nos. LXI and LXXII (London, 1892 and 1897), II, complains at length about the neglect of discharged soldiers (869 ff.), the covetousness of the rich (1177 ff.), the frequency of adultery (1758 ff.), the Privy Seal's reluctance to pay his annuity (1779 ff. and again 4355 ff.), the neglect of worthy clerks of Oxford and Cambridge (5272 ff.), and many equally temporary or personal evils.

2 See T. Wright, ed., Thomas Hoccleve's *De Regimine Principum* (London, 1860), p. xiv.

3 For Chaucer's stylistic borrowings from Geoffrey de Vinsauf's *Nova Poetria* and Boccaccio's *Filostrato*, see J. C. Mendenhall, *Aureate Terms* (Univ. of Pennsylvania, 1919), pp. 41–45.

4 The *OED* cites as the first instance of the term a statement in the prologue of the *Troy Book*: 'And of my penne the tracys to correcte,/Whyche bareyn is of aureat lycour' (30–31). Mendenhall, *Aureate Terms*, p. 7, states that Lydgate introduced the term in the English language, but he gives no supporting evidence. Whether or not Lydgate really introduced the term, he uses it several times in the *Troy Book* and at least once in the *Fall of Princes*.

5 William Dunbar, *Ane Ballat of Our Lady*, in *The Poems of William Dunbar*, ed. J. Schipper (Vienna, 1894), pp. 369–70.

6 Isabel Hyde, 'Lydgate's "Halff Chongyd Latyne": an Illustration', *MLN*, LXX (1955), 252 ff.

7 A. S. Cook, trans., *Vexilla Regis Prodeunt* in L. R. Lind, ed., *Latin Poetry in Verse Translation* (Boston, 1957), p. 331.

8 *Minor Poems*, I, 25–27, line 1.

9 See above, chapter VII, notes 28, 29, and text. For the relationship between the *Mirroure for Magistrates* and the *Fall of Princes* see also L. B. Campbell, *The Mirror for Magistrates* (Cambridge, England, 1938), p. 5, and Schirmer, 'The Importance of the Fifteenth Century', p. 104.

10 For Lydgate's influence upon the diction of Thomas Sackville's contribution to the *Mirroure for Magistrates*, see M. Hearsey, *The Complaint of Henry Duke of Buckingham* (New Haven, 1936), p. 108.

11 For the argument that the *Fall of Princes* contains the source of the Gonzago story in *Hamlet*, see M. Montgomery, 'Lydgate's *Fall of Princes* and *Hamlet*', *TLS*, October 1924, p. 651.

12 E. M. W. Tillyard, *Shakespeare's History Plays* (London, 1948), pp. 72, 129, and *passim*, argues the influence of the *Fall of Princes* on Shakespeare's history plays, especially *Richard II*.

13 E. M. W. Tillyard, *Shakespeare's Problem Plays* (London, 1957), pp. 41 ff. The influence of the *Troy Book* on Shakespeare's *Troilus and Cressida* was first pointed out by G. Steevens, ed., *The Plays of William Shakespeare* (London, 1793), XI, 211. Since that time, it has been minimized by F. Douce, in *Illustrations of Shakespeare and of Ancient Manners* (London, 1807), II, 53; and by W. Blades, *The Life and Typography of William Caxton* (London, 1861–3), II, 15, who argues instead the influence of Caxton's *Recuyell of the Histories of Troy*, and again in *The Biography and Typography of William Caxton* (New York, 1882), p. 172. W. Greif, *Die mittelalterlichen Bearbeitungen der Trojanersage* (Marburg, 1886), merely mentions the *Troy Book* among other sources of *Troilus and Cressida*. Tillyard's argument differs from its predecessors in that it seems to be based on the thorough and thoughtful reading of both the poem and the play.

[14] On the subject of Heywood's authorship, see C. A. Rouse, 'Thomas Heywood and *The Life and Death of Hector*', *PMLA*, XLIII (1928), 779; A. M. Clark, *Thomas Heywood, Playwright and Miscellanist* (Oxford, 1931), p. 340; D. Bush, 'William Painter and Thomas Heywood', *MLN*, LIV (1939), 279. All subsequent references and quotations from the work are to Thomas Purfoot's print (London, 1614).

[15] Tillyard, *English Epic*, p. 202.

INDEX

Adrastus, 118, 128, 129, 131
Aeneas, 96
Aeneid, Virgil, 3, 6, 37, 63, 64
Aeschylus, 19
Aesop, 61
Aethicus, 41
affected modesty, 55, 56, 59, 116
Agincourt, 27, 113, 130
Alcuin, 117
Alexander, 72
Alexanderlied, 37
Amphiorax, 123, 124, 125, 126, 130
Amoryus and Cleopes, John Metham, 1
Ane Ballade of Our Lady, 137
Anelida and Arcite, Chaucer, 50, 68, 111
Anglo-Saxon Chronicle, 35
Anticlaudianus, 138
Aquinas, Saint Thomas, 104
Ariosto, *Orlando Furioso*, 40
Arnold, Matthew, 56
Art Poetique, Boileau, 34
Aristotle, 43, 72, 126
  Politics, 43
Aue, Hartmann von, *Iwein*, 63
Ayers, 127

Bale, John, 4
Ballade at the Reverence of Our Lady, 137
Ballade on ane Ale Seller, 82
Ballade to King Henry VI on his Coronation, 105
Barbour, John, 53, 95
Beaufort, Henry, Bishop of Winchester, 41, 50
Beauvais, de, *Speculum Historiale*, 44
Beccaria, Antonio, 41, 43
Bedier, Joseph, 34
Bern, Dietrich von, 77
Bennett, H. S., *Six Medieval Men and Women*, 1, 9, 41
Beowulf, 35
Beware of Doublenesse, 81
Bible Historiale, Desmoulins, 44
Bibliographica Poetica, 6, 7
Bishop Guy of Valence, 71
Boccaccio, 14, 22, 35, 43, 44, 53, 64, 100, 101, 103, 105
  Filostrate, 35
  de Casibus, 43, 44, 64
  De Casibus Virorum Illustrium, 105
Boileau, 34
  Art Poetique, 34
Bokenham, 43
Bolingbroke, 129
Book of the Duchess, Chaucer, 25, 47, 62, 73
Bracciolini, Poggio, 41, 42, 50, 51
Bronson, Bertrand H., 90
Brown, Carleton, 2
Browning, E. B., 10, 14, 83
  Soliloquy of the Spanish Cloister, 83
Bruce, 53, 95
Bruni, Leonardo, 43
Brut, Layamon, 95
Brutus, 96

Caesar, 39, 41, 105
Candido, Pier, 43
Canterbury Tales, Chaucer, 2, 111, 113, 114, 116, 130

Capella, Martianus, 41
Capellaunus, Andreas, 77, 80
Castiglione, *Courtier*, 40, 103, 104
Caxton, William, 2, 3, 36, 37
Cessolis, Jacobus de, 68
Chalmers, Alexander, 27, 28
Chanson de Roland, 26, 67, 75
Chapman, *Homer*, 35
Chartier, Alain, 96
Chastelaine de Vergy, 76
Chaucer, 2, 3, 4, 5, 6, 7, 8, 11, 25, 28, 29, 30, 31, 35, 36, 38, 40, 43, 44, 46, 47, 48, 49, 50, 51, 52, 55, 56, 57, 58, 60, 62, 64, 68, 69, 72, 79, 80, 87, 102, 124, 126, 134, 142, 143
Chaucer, John Stowe, 2
Chronicle, Robert of Gloucester, 95
Churl and the Bird, 44, 50, 52, 54
Cibber, Theophilus, 5
Cicero, 32, 41, 116
Claudian, 34
Col, Gonthier, 79
Comestor, Peter, 68
Commonwealth, 5
Companho Faray Un Vers Covinen, 85
Complaint of the Black Knight, 24, 28, 46, 47, 48, 49, 61, 84, 85
Complaint to his Purse, 129
Confessio Amantis, Gower, 21, 53, 141
Continental Literature, 1
Cook, Albert, 138
Cook's Tale, 113
Cooper, Elizabeth, 9
Courthope, W. J., 30
Courtier, Castiglione, 40, 103, 104
courtly love, 78–79, 83
Crist O/E, 19
  cf. *Testament* p. 18, lines 754–761
criticism in 15th century, 14
Curtius, 73, 117
Coleridge, S. T., 14
Colet, John, 40
Colonne, Guido delle, 11, 38, 44, 52, 62, 64, 66, 67
  Historia Destructionis Trojae, 38, 44

Dante, 34, 75, 102, 126
  Monarchim, 103, 104
Debate of the Horse, Sheep, and Goose, 101
De Cas et Ruine des Nobles Hommes et Femmes, 105
De Casibus Virorum Illustrium, Boccaccio, 22, 105
De Claris Mulieribus, Boccaccio, 44
De Conjuge non Ducenda, 80
defenders, obscurity of, 14
de Deguileville, Guillaume, *Pelerinage de la Vie Humaine*, 64
Delphic Oracle, 70
Denomy, Father A. J., 83, 84
De Regimine Principium, 103, 104
Des Cas des Nobles Hommes et Femmes, 64
De la Ruyne des Nobles Hommes et Femmes, 105
Des Nobles Malheureux, 105
Deschamps, 78
Desmoulins, Guyart, *Bible Historiale*, 44
Diogenes, 126
Disciplina Clericalis, 44
Dit du Bleu Chevalier, Froissart, 50
Dido, 63
Dickens, *Great Expectations*, 18
  Pickwick Papers, 33
dignity, human, 74–76
  as important theme in Renaissance, 142
Dioscorides, 41
Discourse on English Poetry, A, William Webbe, 4
D'Israeli, Isaac, 6, 7, 29
disrepute (of Lydgate) in nineteenth century, 6–8
Donaldson, E. Talbot, 90
Donne, John, 27
Douglas, Gavin, 35, 36, 37, 38, 39, 40, 67
Dryden, 36, 38, 102
Du Bellay, Joachim, 39
Dunbar, William, 137
Dürer, Albrecht, 34

Ekwall, 30
Elizabeth I, 95
  Court of, 128
Ellis, George, 13
Elyot, Thomas, 91, 103
  Defense of Good Women, 91
Eneados, Gavin Douglas, 36, 37, 39, 40, 67
Engelhard, Konrad von Wurzburg, 93
Engellant, Ritschiert von, 93
Engeltrut in *Engelhard*, 93
England, Trojan origins of, 96

English Anthology, Chaucer, 29
English Language, criticism of, 139, 140
English Literature, paucity of in Lydgate's time, 3
Eolus, *Fall of Princes*, 20
Erasmus, *Praise of Folly*, 40
De Matrimonio Christiano, 91
Erdmann, Axel, 27, 30
Eschenbach, von, *Parzival*, 52, 75 ff.
Euphuism, 137
Eutropius, 30
Examples against Women, 80

Farnham, Willard, 66, 92, 138
Fabula Duorum Mercatorum, 53
Faerie Queene, Spenser, 50, 74, 127, 132
Fall of Princes, 2, 6, 8, 14, 20 ff., 21, 44, 53, 54, 58, 59, 64, 68, 71, 72, 88, 89, 90, 92, 100, 106, 107, 108, 109, 110, 111
favourable critics in the nineteenth century, 9
Filostrate, Boccaccio, 35, 36
first adverse criticism, 6
Flemmyng, Robert, 42
Floure of Courtesy, 23 ff., 28, 50, 86
Flower and the Leaf, 40
France, war with, 113
Free, John, 42
Froissart, Jehan, *Dit du Bleu Chevalier*, 50, 79
Frulovisi, Tito Livio, 43

Gentlewoman's Lament, 56
Gest Historiale of the Destruction of Troy, 38, 39, 66, 111
Gesta Romanorum, 31, 43, 44
Gormont et Isembart, 76
Gosse, Edmund, 9
Governaunce of Kynges and Prynces, 108
Governor, 103, 104
Gower, 3, 5, 21, 53, 104, 141
Confessio Amantis, 21, 53, 141
Vox Clamantis, 104
Gray, 6, 13, 14, 16, 17, 19, 21
On the Poems of Lydgate, 6
Great Expectations, Dickens, 18
Greece, ancient, 16, 17, 37
Greeks, ancient, 38
Grey, William, 42
Grocyn, William, 40
Gunthorpe, John, 42
Guy of Warwyck, 11, 53

Hales, Thomas de, *Love Run*, 62
Hamlet, 74, 103, 104, 138
Hartmann, 64
Hastings, battle of, 35
Hazard, Paul, 34
Hawes, Stephen, 15, 41
Pastime of Pleasure, 3, 41
Hector, 97, 98, 99
Henry II, 34
IV, 42, 43
V, 43, 53, 130
VI, 134, 139
VII, 3
Heroides, comparison with, 22
Heroides, Ovid, 22, 23
Heywood, Thomas, *Iron Age*, 5, 138
Hildebrand, 96
Hildebrandslied, 96
Historia Destructionis Trojae, Guido delle Colonne, 38, 44, 66, 67
History of English Literature, Legouis & Cazamian, 15
History of King Richard III, 40
Hoccleve, Thomas, 40, 43, 136
Homer, 6, 16, 17, 66, 67, 71, 97, 99, 140
Homer, Chapman's, 35
Horace, 14, 41
House of Fame, 50, 55, 63
comic tone in, 55
humanism, 33
Hugo, H. E., 34
Huizinga, Johan, 33, 34
human suffering, depictions of, 17–19
Humphrey, Duke of Gloucester, 40, 42, 43, 71, 72, 92, 103, 106
Hyde, Isabel, 137

Iliad, the, 17
imitation, 57, 58
individualism, 93–94
Insulis, Alanus de, 138
Iron Age, Thomas Heywood, 5, 138
Isodore of Seville, 68
Isopes Fabules, 50, 53, 54, 61
Iwein, von Aue, 63

Jocasta, 117 ff.
John of Gaunt, 102

John of Salisbury, *Policratus*, 103, 104, 106
Justin, 41
Juvenal, 41

King John of France, 100
Kingship, attitudes towards, 106–108
Kings of England Sithen William Conqueror, 97
Knight's Tale, 47, 111, 114, 116, 131
Knox, John, *First Blast of the Trumpet against the Monstrous Regiment of Women*, 91

Laius, 118
Lane, John, 113
Lawson, John, *Orchet*, 4
Layamon, *Brut*, 95
Lay of Sir Orfeo, 37
Legend of Good Women, Chaucer, 2, 47, 78, 87
Legouis & Cazamian, 15
Lewis, C. Day, 38
Lewis, C. S., 34, 35
Lichtenstein, Ulrich von, *Frauendeinst*, 78
Life and Death of Hector, The, 138, 139, 140
Life of Our Lady, 11, 19 ff., 21, 28, 57
Linacre, Thomas, *Rudimenta Grammatica*, 40
Literary History of England A. C. Baugh, 15, 16
Livy, 30
Locke, F. W., 77
Lollius, 52
Lord Mayor of London, 2
Lounsbury, Thomas, 10, 11, 13, 14, 15
Lounsbury and Saintsbury, shortcomings of judgement of, 14
love, penances in, 57
Lydgate, as poet in transition, 143
  as poet of 15th century, 143
  as translator, 64–67
Lyly, William, 40

Macbeth, 134, 137
MacCracken, Henry Noble, 27, 30, 112
Machaut, Guillaume de, 50, 79
Machiavelli, *Prince*, 40, 103, 104
Mackail, J. W., 38
Macrobius, 41
Magnificence, Skelton, 40
Manutius, Aldus, 40
Marie de France, 50
Maximus, Valerius, 41
medieval qualities in Lydgate, 60, 136
Melville, *Moby Dick*, 17
Metham, John, 137
  Amoryus and Cleopes, 1
Meung, J., 79, 86
Middle Ages, 1, 31, 32, 35, 38, 39, 44, 46, 51, 60, 61, 71, 72, 73, 75, 76, 77, 84, 86
Middle English, 14, 35
Milton, 52, 56, 74, 127, 143
  Paradise Lost, 52, 74, 127
Minot, Laurence, 95
Mirrour for Magistrates, 108, 138
Moby Dick, Melville, 17
Modern critics embarrassed by Lydgate, 11, 12, 56
Monarchia, Dante, 103, 104
monastic influence, 83, 84, 85
Monk's Tale, Chaucer, 44, 111
Monte, Piero del, 42
Montreuil, Jehan de, 79
More, Thomas, *History of King Richard III*, 40
  Utopia, 40
Mumming at Windsor, 72
Mumming for the Mercers of London, 72
Muscatine, Charles, 35
Muses Mercury, the, 5

Narrative technique, 59
Nash, Ogden, 34, 41
nationalism, medieval, 102–103
Nativity, 19
New World, 14
Nibelunglied, Wagner, 26, 52, 77, 96, 117
Nördstrom, Johan, 32
Norman Conquest, 35, 95

Occleve, 5, 6, 9
Oedipus, 5, 117, 118, 119, 120, 121, 122, 131
  appeal of, to Middle Ages, 134
Of Her That Hath All Virtues, 83
Old English, 35

Orchet, John Lawson, 4
Orlando Furioso, Ariosto, 40
Ormulum, 35
Ovid, 22, 23, 68, 69
  Heroides, 22, 23
  attitude to, 68
Ovide Moralise, 37, 73
Oxford Presses, 42

Pain and Sorrow of Evil Marriage, 80
Painter, Sidney, 96
Panofsky, Erwin, 32, 37, 40
Pantagruel, Rabelais, 40
Paradise Lost, Milton, 52, 74, 127
paradox, use of, 21
Parliament of Fowls, Chaucer, 2, 50, 73
Parliament of Three Ages, 36
Pastime of Pleasure, Stephen Hawes, 3
patronage, 111
Peacham, Henry, 8
Pearl, 36
Percy, Thomas, 6, 7, 13, 16, 27, 29, 56
  Reliques of Ancient Poetry, 6
Persius, 40
Petrarch, 32, 102
Petworth, Richard, 41
Piers Plowman, 36, 104
Plautus, 41
Pliny, 39, 41
Poema Morale, 16, 60
Pole, William de la, 8
Policraticus, John of Salisbury, 103, 104
Politics, Aristotle, 43
Polybus, 118
Pompey, 105
Praise of Folly, Erasmus, 40, 41
Printed editions, 2
Ptolemy of Lucca, 104
Prince, Machiavelli, 40, 103, 104
prolixity, 16–17
Prometheus Bound, 19
Proust, *Memories of Things Past*, 17
Puttenham, George, 5
Pynson, Richard, 2

Quadrilogue Inventif, 96
Quintilian, 41

Rabelais, *Pantagruel*, 40
Raoul de Cambrai, 63, 76
Reformation, 4
Regement of Princes, 136
reputation in Lydgate's own time, 2, 3, 4, 5
  in 15th and 16th centuries, 5, 6
Renaissance, 1, 3, 4, 31, 32, 33, 34, 35, 37, 39, 40, 41, 42, 43, 44, 45, 51, 61, 71, 72, 74, 86, 134, 136, 142
  Continental, 40
  English, 40, 74, 134, 136, 142
  Italian, 41, 42
Rheims, Cathedral of, 40
Richard II, 102
Ritson, Joseph, 6, 7, 9, 10, 13, 15, 16, 17, 27, 28, 29, 30, 56
  Bibliographica Poetica, 6, 7
Robbins, Rossell Hope, 1
Robert of Gloucester, *Chronicle*, 95
Robert of Sicily, 104
Romance of the Rose, 44, 47, 50, 86, 87
Roman de Aeneas, 36
Roman de Edipus, 117, 119
  comparison with *Siege of Thebes*, 119–135
Roman de Troy, 37
Romantics, 34
Rome, 38
Rousillon, Girard de, 76
Rudimenta Grammatica, Thomas Linacre, 40

Sackville, Thomas, 138
Saint Augustine, 36
Saint Bernard, 77, 80
  De Cura Rei Famuliaris, 80
Sainte More, Benoit de, 68
Saint Joan, 100
Saintsbury, George, 10, 11, 14, 15, 43
  The Cambridge History of English Literature, 11, 12
Salisbury, John of, 39
Sallust, 41
Sampson, George, 15
sapientia et fortitudes, Ideal of, 129
Schatzkammer Gospels, 40
Schick, Joseph, 31, 56
Schirmer, Walter F., 3, 10, 40
Scogan, 43
Scott, Mary Augusta, 9
Seaton, Ethel, 9
Secrees of Old Philosòffres, 54, 71, 72, 108, 136
Secreta Secretorum, 108, 126

Siege of Thebes, 2, 7, 25 ff., 27, 28, 30, 53, 59, 73, 104, 110, 113, 114, 116, 117, 119, 125, 126, 127, 128, 129, 130, 131, 133, 134, 138, 142
attitude to kingship in, 127
division of presentation of material in, 119, 120, 121, 122
worship of pagan gods in, 121
moral message in, 126–127
nationalistic spirit of, 134
Seneca, 41, 126
Serpent Division, 30, 105
Servius, 41
Seznec, Jean, 38
Shakespeare, 16, 52, 74, 76, 102, 138
Shaw, George Bernard, 74, 100, 141
Sherry, Richard, *Treatise of Schemes and Tropes*, 4
Sidney, Sir Philip, 131
Sir Gawain and the Green Knight, 26
Six Medieval Men and Women, H. S. Bennett, 1
Skelton, John, 3, 8, 15, 40
Magnificence, 40
Socrates, 126
Solinus, 41
Speculum Historiale, de Beauvais, 44
Spenser, 50, 51, 74, 127, 132
Faerie Queene, 50, 74, 127, 132
Sphinx, 120
Squire's Tale, 50, 113
Statius, *Thebaid*, 30, 41, 113
Stowe, John, *Chaucer*, 2
Stylistic weakness, 139

Tacitus, 39
Tale of Beryn, 113
Tale of Meribee, 126
Tale of the Wolfe and the Lamb, 92
Temple of Glas, 2, 50, 93
Testament, 7
Thebaid, Statius, 30, 41, 113
Thompson, Richard, 9
Tillyard, E. M. W., 36, 74, 76, 138
Tottell, Richard, 2
Towris, 38
Treatise of Schemes and Tropes, Sherry, 4
Treaty of Troyes, 134
Troilus and Criseyde, Chaucer, 2, 35, 47, 48, 52, 73, 111, 125, 134, 138
Trojan Ancestors of England, 99–100
Trojan war, 66
Troy, 37, 38
Troy Book, 5, 11, 12, 52, 54, 56, 57, 58, 59, 62, 66, 67, 68, 71, 72, 82, 86, 87, 89, 92, 96, 100, 104, 110, 112, 113, 114, 136, 138, 141, 142
influences on, 68, 69, 70
Troyes, Chrestien de, *Cliges*, 52
Yvain, 63
Turner, Sharon, 7
Tydeus, 118, 119, 129, 130, 131, 133

Utley, 77, 90, 91, 102
Utopia, *More*, 40

Vasari, 34
Venantius Fortunatus, *Vexilla Regis Prodeunt*, 138
Victorian Period, 33
Villani, Filippo, 33, 34
Villon, 34
Virgil, 36, 38, 39, 41, 50, 68, 69
Aeneid, adaptations of, 63
Virgin Mary, 19
Vitruvius, 41
Vives, *De Institutione Christianae Feminae*, 91
Vox Clamantis, 104

Walsingham, Thomas, 42
Warton, Thomas, 5, 14, 16
Webbe, William, *A Discourse on English Poetry*, 4
Weiss, Roberto, 41
Whethamstede, John, 42
'Wiedererwaschung', 34
Wife of Bath (quote), 78
William the Conqueror, 35
William IX of Aquitaine, 85, 86
Worde, Wynkyn de, 2
women, attitudes towards, 76–78, 79–83
defences of, 90–92
generalizations about, 88, 89
infidelity in, 88, 89
Wurzburg, Konrad von, *Engelhard*, 93